PRENTICE HALL

SCIENCE EXPLORER

Focus on
Life Science

Student Edition

Guided Reading and Study Workbook

CALIFORNIA EDITION

Prentice Hall

PRENTICE HALL
Needham, Massachusetts
Upper Saddle River, New Jersey
Glenview, Illinois

Student Edition ISBN 0-13-052728-9
10   06 05 04 03

Table of Contents

© Prentice-Hall, Inc.

TABLE OF CONTENTS *(continued)*

Science Explorer *Focus on Life Science*

CHAPTER 1

CELL STRUCTURE AND FUNCTION

....

SECTION 1-1 **Discovering Cells** (pages 6-12)

This section describes how the invention of the microscope led to the development of a theory on cells. The section also explains how a light microscope works.

▶ Introduction (pages 6–7)

1. What are cells? _____

_____

▶ First Sightings of Cells (page 7)

2. What did the invention of the microscope make possible? _____

_____

3. An instrument that makes small objects look larger is a(n)

_____.

4. Is the following sentence true or false? A compound microscope has only

one lens. _____

5. Complete the following table about the first people to observe cells.

The First People to Observe Cells		
Questions	Robert Hooke	Anton van Leeuwenhoek
What kind of microscope did he use?		
What did he first look at with the microscope?		
What did he name what he saw?		

© Prentice-Hall, Inc.

CHAPTER 1, Cell Structure and Function *(continued)*

▶ The Cell Theory (page 10)

6. Is the following sentence true or false? Theodor Schwann worked alone

   to develop the cell theory. _____

7. List the three points of the cell theory.

   a. _____

   b. _____

   c. _____

▶ How a Light Microscope Works (pages 11–12)

8. Is the following sentence true or false? Magnification is the ability to

   make things look larger than they are. _____

9. How do the lenses of a light microscope make an object look larger?

   _____

   _____

10. In a convex lens, the _____ of the lens is thicker than the

    _____.

11. What is resolution? _____

    _____

    _____

▶ Electron Microscopes (page 12)

12. A microscope that uses a beam of electrons to examine a specimen is

    called a(n) _____.

13. Circle the letter of the microscope that has better resolution.

    a. light microscope

    b. electron microscope

SECTION 1-2 Looking Inside Cells (pages 13-21)

This section describes cell structure and function in plant cells, animal cells, and bacteria.

▶ Introduction (pages 13–14)

1. What are organelles? _____

_____

▶ Cell Wall (page 14)

2. The rigid layer of nonliving material that surrounds plant cells is the

_____.

3. Circle the letter of each sentence that is true about the cell wall.

   a. Cell walls are made of cellulose.

   b. Plant cells have cell walls.

   c. Animal cells have cell walls.

   d. Water and oxygen cannot pass through the cell wall.

4. What does the cell wall do? _____

_____

▶ Cell Membrane (pages 14–15)

5. Where is the cell membrane located in cells that have cell walls?

_____

6. Where is the cell membrane located in cells that do NOT have cell walls?

_____

_____

7. Is the following sentence true or false? The main function of the cell

   membrane is to control what comes into and out of a cell. _____

© Prentice-Hall, Inc.

CHAPTER 1, Cell Structure and Function (continued)

▶ Nucleus (pages 15–18)

8. Circle the letter of each sentence that is true about the nucleus.

   a. Materials move into the nucleus through pores in the nuclear membrane.

   b. Chromatin contains the instructions that direct the functions of a cell.

   c. The nucleolus is part of the nuclear membrane.

   d. Ribosomes are made in the nucleolus.

▶ Organelles in the Cytoplasm (pages 18–20)

9. Circle the letter of the part of the cell that is the region between the cell membrane and the nucleus.

   a. organelle   b. nucleus   c. cytoplasm   d. chromatin

10. In the table below, describe the function of each organelle in the cytoplasm.

Organelles in Cytoplasm	
Organelle	Function
Mitochondria	
Endoplasmic reticulum	
Ribosomes	
Golgi bodies	
Chloroplasts	
Vacuoles	
Lysosomes	

© Prentice-Hall, Inc.

▶ Bacterial Cells (page 20)

11. Circle the letter of each sentence that is true about bacterial cells.

    a. Bacterial cells are larger than plant or animal cells.

    b. Bacterial cells have a cell wall and a cell membrane.

    c. Bacterial cells do not have a nucleus.

    d. Bacterial cells do not have genetic material.

▶ Specialized Cells (page 21)

12. The structure of each kind of body cell is suited to its _____.

· ·

SECTION 1-3 Chemical Compounds in Cells
(pages 23-27)

This section identifies the basic building blocks of cells. It also explains the importance of water to cells.

▶ Elements and Compounds (page 23)

1. A(n) _____ is any substance that cannot be broken down

    into simpler substances. Its smallest unit is the _____.

2. When two or more elements combine chemically, they form a

    _____. Its smallest unit is called a(n) _____.

▶ Organic and Inorganic Compounds (page 24)

3. Complete this concept map on organic compounds.

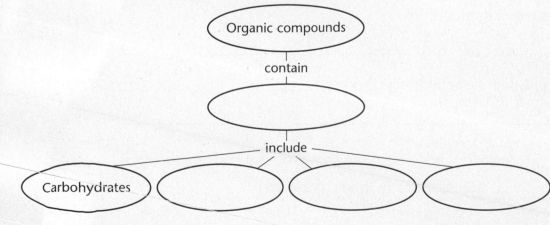

CHAPTER 1, Cell Structure and Function (continued)

4. Compounds that do not contain carbon are called _____.

▶ Carbohydrates (page 24)

5. An energy-rich organic compound made of carbon, hydrogen, and

   oxygen is a(n) _____.

6. Starch is a kind of carbohydrate. What foods have starch? _____

   _____

   _____

7. How do cells use carbohydrates? _____

   _____

   _____

▶ Proteins (page 25)

8. _____ form parts of cell membranes and many of the
   cell's organelles.

9. What small molecules make up proteins? _____

10. What do enzymes do? _____

    _____

    _____

▶ Lipids (page 26)

11. What are three examples of lipids?

    a. _____ b. _____ c. _____

12. How are lipids like carbohydrates? _____

    _____

    _____

13. Cells store _____ in lipids to use later.

▶ Nucleic Acids (pages 26–27)

14. Very large organic molecules that contain instructions that cells need to

function are called _____ .

15. Is the following sentence true or false? Nucleic acids have the instructions

that cells need to carry out all life functions. _____

16. List the two kinds of nucleic acids.

a. _____

b. _____

▶ Water and Living Things (page 27)

17. List four ways that cells use water.

a. _____

_____

b. _____

_____

c. _____

_____

d. _____

_____

Reading Skill Practice

Making a table can help you organize the information you have read. Make a table to organize what you have learned about the chemical compounds in cells. The title of the table should be *Chemical Compounds in Cells.* The five column heads should be *Compound, Organic or Inorganic, Elements It's Made Of, Job in the Cell,* and *Foods It's Found In.* The five row heads should be *Carbohydrates, Proteins, Lipids, Nucleic Acids,* and *Water.* Do your work on a separate sheet of paper. For more information about tables, see page 766 in your textbook.

CHAPTER 1, Cell Structure and Function *(continued)*

● ●

SECTION 1-4 **The Cell in Its Environment**
(pages 30-34)

This section tells how things move into and out of cells.

▶ **The Cell Membrane as Gatekeeper** (page 30)

1. The cell membrane is _____, which means that some things can pass through it while others cannot.

2. List three ways that substances can move into and out of a cell.

    a. _____

    b. _____

    c. _____

▶ **Diffusion—Molecules in Motion** (page 31)

3. In diffusion, molecules move from an area of _____

    concentration to an area of _____ concentration.

4. Draw molecules on Part B of the diagram below to show how the molecules are distributed inside and outside the cell after diffusion has occurred.

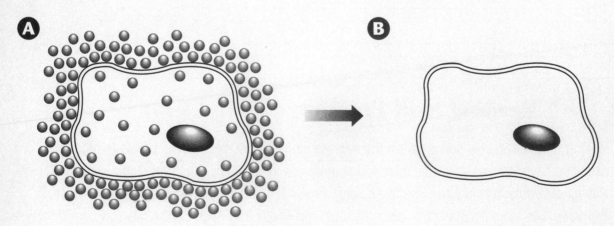

Science Explorer Focus on Life Science

▶ Osmosis—The Diffusion of Water Molecules (page 32)

5. In _____, water molecules diffuse through a selectively permeable membrane.

Match the shape of each red blood cell with the concentration of water it is floating in. See Figure 17 on page 32.

Shape of Cell	Kind of Water
_____ **6.** normal	**a.** Low concentration of water molecules outside the cell
_____ **7.** shrunken	**b.** Concentration of water molecules is the same inside and outside of the cell
_____ **8.** swollen	**c.** High concentration of water molecules outside the cell

▶ Active Transport (pages 33–34)

9. Two ways of moving things into and out of cells that do NOT need

   energy are _____. Moving materials through a

   cell membrane without using energy is called _____

   transport.

10. How does active transport differ from passive transport?

   _____

   _____

   _____

11. List two ways that the cell moves things by active transport.

   a. _____

   b. _____

▶ Why Are Cells Small? (page 34)

12. Is the following sentence true or false? As a cell gets larger, it takes longer

   for a molecule to reach the middle of the cell. _____

CHAPTER 1, Cell Structure and Function *(continued)*

Word Wise

Match each definition on the left with the correct term on the right. Then write the number of each term in the appropriate box below. When you have filled in all the boxes, add up the numbers in each column, row, and two diagonals. The sums should be the same. Some terms may not be used.

A. Acts as the cell's control center

B. Area between the cell membrane and the nucleus

C. The movement of materials through a cell membrane without using energy

D. An energy-rich compound such as sugar

E. Basic unit of structure and function in living things

F. Process by which molecules move from an area of higher concentration to one of lower concentration

G. Make things look larger than they are

H. Genetic material in the nucleus

I. Protein that speeds up chemical reactions

1. cytoplasm
2. active transport
3. magnification
4. enzyme
5. diffusion
6. cell
7. carbohydrate
8. nucleus
9. passive transport
10. resolution
11. chromatin
12. lipid

A _____	B _____	C _____
D _____	E _____	F _____
G _____	H _____	I _____

= _____

= _____

= _____

= _____

=   =   =

_____ _____ _____

= _____

CHAPTER 2
CELL PROCESSES AND ENERGY

. . . .

SECTION 2–1 Photosynthesis
(pages 40–44)

This section explains how plants make food by using the energy from sunlight.

▶ What Is Photosynthesis? (page 41)

1. In the process of photosynthesis, plants use the energy from

   _____ to make food.

▶ A Two-Stage Process (pages 41–42)

2. List the two stages in the process of photosynthesis.

   a. _____

   b. _____

3. The green pigment in chloroplasts, called _____, absorbs
   light energy from the sun.

4. Is the following sentence true or false? Besides the energy from sunlight,

   the cell needs water and carbon dioxide to make sugar. _____

5. What are stomata? _____

   _____

6. Circle the letter of each product of photosynthesis.
   a. water   **b.** carbon dioxide   **c.** oxygen   **d.** sugars

▶ The Photosynthesis Equation (page 43)

7. Write the chemical equation for the process of photosynthesis.

   _____

CHAPTER 2, Cell Processes and Energy *(continued)*

8. What word does the arrow in the chemical equation stand for?

_____

9. Circle the letter of each raw material of photosynthesis.

    a. carbon dioxide   **b.** glucose

    c. water   **d.** oxygen

10. Circle the letter of each sentence that is true about the products of photosynthesis.

    a. Plant cells use the sugar for food.

    b. Some of the sugar is made into other compounds, such as cellulose.

    c. Some of the sugar is stored in the plant's cells for later use.

    d. Extra sugar molecules pass out of the plant through the stomata.

▶ Photosynthesis and Life (page 44)

11. Complete the following table about how living things use the sun's energy.

How Living Things Use Energy From the Sun		
Living Thing	**Autotroph or Heterotroph?**	**Obtains Energy From the Sun Directly or Indirectly?**
Plant		
Caterpillar		
Bluebird		

12. Is the following sentence true or false? Photosynthesis produces the carbon dioxide that most living things need to survive. _____

📖 Reading Skill Practice

Writing a summary can help you remember the important ideas of what you have read. Write a summary of the process of photosynthesis. Your summary should be much shorter than the text on which it is based. Do your work on a separate sheet of paper.

SECTION 2-2 Respiration (pages 45-49)

In this section, you will learn how cells get energy from food.

▶ Storing and Releasing Energy (page 46)

1. Cells store energy in the form of _____.

2. How do cells get energy? _____

_____

▶ Respiration (pages 46–47)

3. What happens during respiration? _____

_____

_____

_____

4. Is the following sentence true or false? Respiration that takes place inside
of cells is the same as breathing air in and out of the lungs.

_____

5. Is the following sentence true or false? The most efficient means of
obtaining energy from glucose requires the presence of carbon dioxide.

_____

6. Use the table below to list the raw materials and products of respiration.

Respiration	
Raw Materials	**Products**

CHAPTER 2, Cell Processes and Energy *(continued)*

Match the events in respiration with the stages in which they occur. The items in the second column may be used more than once.

Event in Respiration	Stage of Process
_____ 7. Takes place in the mitochondria	**a.** first stage
_____ 8. Takes place in the cytoplasm	**b.** second stage
_____ 9. Oxygen is involved.	**c.** both first and second stage
_____ 10. Energy is released.	
_____ 11. Glucose molecules are broken down.	

▶ Comparing Photosynthesis and Respiration (page 48)

12. Complete the cycle diagram below, which describes the relationship between photosynthesis and respiration. See Figure 7 on page 48.

Photosynthesis   **Respiration**

Plants produce _____.

Animals use _____.

Plants use _____.

Animals produce _____.

▶ Fermentation (pages 48–49)

13. What is fermentation? _____

_____

14. Is the following sentence true or false? Fermentation releases more

energy than respiration. _____

15. List the two types of fermentation and tell where each takes place.

a. _____

_____

b. _____

_____

. . . .

SECTION 2-3 Cell Division (pages 51-58)

This section explains how cells grow and divide.

▶ The Cell Cycle (page 52)

1. The regular sequence of growth and division that cells undergo is called

the _____.

▶ Stage 1: Interphase (pages 52–53)

2. List three things that the cell is doing during interphase.

a. _____

b. _____

c. _____

3. Circle the letter of the process in which the cell copies its DNA.

a. interphase   b. cell cycle   c. replication   d. division

▶ Stage 2: Mitosis (pages 53–55)

4. Circle the letter of each sentence that is true about mitosis.

a. The cell makes a copy of its DNA.

b. The cell divides into two new cells.

c. The cell's nucleus divides into two new nuclei.

d. One copy of DNA is divided between both daughter cells.

CHAPTER 2, Cell Processes and Energy *(continued)*

Match the phases of mitosis with the events that occur in each. See
Exploring the Cell Cycle on pages 54–55.

Event   **Phase**

_____ 5. The centromeres split and the   **a.** prophase
          chromatids separate.
                                                             b. metaphase
_____ 6. The chromatin condenses to form
          chromosomes.   **c.** anaphase

_____ 7. A new nuclear membrane forms around   **d.** telophase
          each set of chromatids.

_____ 8. The chromosomes line up across the center
          of the cell.

9. Label the parts of the structure in the diagram below.

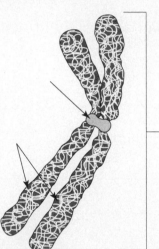

▶ Stage 3: Cytokinesis (page 56)

10. During cytokinesis the _____ divides and the organelles
    are divided between the two new cells.

11. Is the following sentence true or false? During cytokinesis in plant cells,
    the new cell membrane forms before the new cell wall does.

    _____

▶ Length of the Cell Cycle (page 56)

12. Is the following sentence true or false? All cells have a cell cycle that

    lasts the same amount of time? _____

13. Look at the circle graph in Figure 11 on page 56. How long is

interphase in a human liver cell? _____

▶ DNA Replication (pages 57–58)

14. Why does a cell make a copy of its DNA before mitosis occurs?

_____

_____

15. Circle the letter of each molecule that makes up the sides of the DNA ladder.

a. deoxyribose   **b.** glucose   **c.** phosphate   **d.** nitrogen

16. Name the nitrogen bases that pair up to make up the rungs of the DNA ladder.

a. _____ pairs with _____.

b. _____ pairs with _____.

17. Complete the flowchart to show what happens during DNA replication.

DNA Replication

The two sides of the DNA molecule

_____ and _____.

↓

Nitrogen bases floating in the nucleus pair up with the

_____ on each half of the DNA

molecule.

↓

When the new bases are attached, two new

_____ are formed.

CHAPTER 2, Cell Processes and Energy (continued)

· ·

SECTION 2-4 **Cancer** (pages 60-63)

This section explains what happens when cells grow out of control.

▶ What Is Cancer? (pages 61–62)

1. What is cancer? _____

_____

2. Circle the letter of each event that can cause cancer to begin.

   a. A cell divides normally.

   b. A change in DNA affects the cell cycle.

   c. A cell divides too often.

   d. A cell stops dividing.

3. Complete the flowchart below, which describes how cancer begins and spreads.

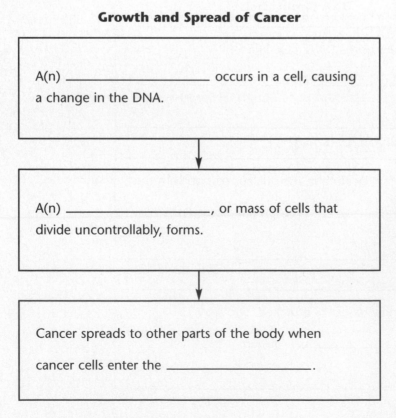

Growth and Spread of Cancer

A(n) _____ occurs in a cell, causing a change in the DNA.

↓

A(n) _____, or mass of cells that divide uncontrollably, forms.

↓

Cancer spreads to other parts of the body when

cancer cells enter the _____.

▶ Treating Cancer (pages 62–63)

4. How can a mutation affect the function of cells? _____

_____

_____

5. Is the following sentence true or false? DNA contains all the

instructions necessary for life. _____

6. List three ways in which doctors usually treat cancer.

a. _____

b. _____

c. _____

7. Why is radiation used to treat cancer? _____

_____

_____

_____

8. Why is chemotherapy an effective way to treat cancer? _____

_____

_____

▶ Cancer Prevention (page 63)

9. Name two things that can cause cancer. _____

_____

_____

10. What kind of diet can help lower a person's risk of some kinds of cancer?

_____

_____

_____

CHAPTER 2, Cell Processes and Energy *(continued)*

WordWise

Answer the clues to solve the crossword puzzle.

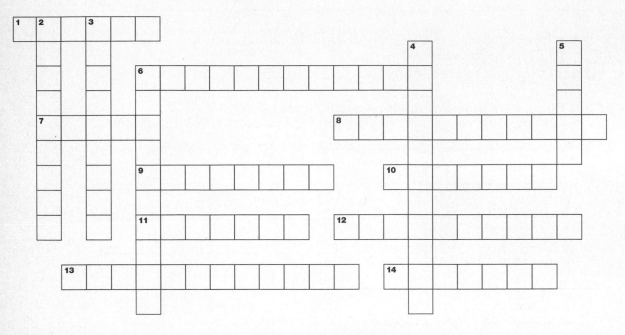

Clues down

2. An organism that makes its own food

3. An individual strand of a chromosome

4. The final stage of the cell cycle in which the cytoplasm divides

5. The regular sequence of growth and division that cells undergo is the cell _____.

6. Condensed genetic material, or chromatin, that is double stranded

Clues across

1. A disease in which cells grow and divide uncontrollably

6. The use of drugs to kill cancer cells

7. A mass of abnormal cells

8. A pigment found in chloroplasts

9. A change in DNA

10. Colored chemical compound in plants that absorbs light

11. Openings on the undersides of leaves

12. The first stage of the cell cycle in which the cell prepares to divide

13. A process by which cells get energy from food without using oxygen

14. The stage of the cell cycle in which the cell's nucleus divides

CHAPTER 3

GENETICS: THE SCIENCE OF HEREDITY

....

SECTION 3-1 **Mendel's Work**
(pages 70-75)

This section describes how Gregor Mendel identified the method by which characteristics are passed from parents to their offspring.

▶ Introduction (page 70)

1. Gregor Mendel experimented with thousands of pea plants to

   understand the process of _____.

Match the term with its definition.

Term	Definition
_____ 2. heredity	**a.** The scientific study of heredity
_____ 3. genetics	**b.** Physical characteristics
_____ 4. traits	**c.** The passing of traits from parents to offspring

▶ Mendel's Peas (pages 70–71)

5. Circle the letter of the characteristic in pea plants that make them good for studying the passing of traits from parent to offspring.

   a. Peas produce small numbers of offspring.

   b. Peas readily cross-pollinate in nature.

   c. Peas have many traits that exist in only two forms.

   d. Peas do not have stamens.

6. In a flower, the female sex cells, or eggs, are produced by the

   _____. The male sex cells, or pollen, are produced by the

   _____.

CHAPTER 3, Genetics: The Science of Heredity *(continued)*

▶ Mendel's Experiments (pages 71–72)

7. Why did Mendel use purebred plants in his experiments? _____

_____

_____

8. Complete the flowchart below, which summarizes Mendel's first experiment with pea plants.

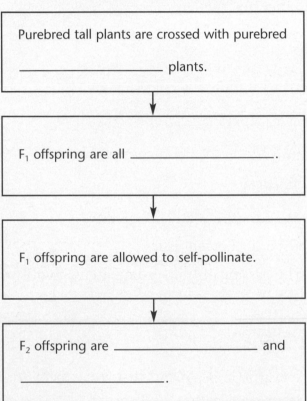

Mendel's Experiment

Purebred tall plants are crossed with purebred

_____ plants.

F₁ offspring are all _____.

F₁ offspring are allowed to self-pollinate.

F₂ offspring are _____ and

_____.

▶ Other Traits (page 72)

9. Circle the letter of other traits in garden peas that Mendel studied. Look at Figure 3 on page 73.

   a. seed size, seed shape, seed color

   b. seed color, pod color, flower color

   c. flower size, pod shape, seed coat color

   d. pod color, seed shape, flower position

10. Two forms of the trait of seed shape in pea plants are

_____ and _____.

▶ Dominant and Recessive Alleles (page 73)

11. Circle the letter of each sentence that is true about alleles.

   a. Genes are factors that control traits.

   b. Alleles are different forms of a gene.

   c. Dominant alleles always show up in the organism when the allele is present.

   d. Recessive alleles mask dominant alleles.

12. Is the following sentence true or false? Only pea plants that have two

recessive alleles for short stems will be short. _____

▶ Understanding Mendel's Crosses (page 74)

Match the pea plant with its combination of alleles.

Pea Plant	Combination of Alleles
_____ **13.** purebred short	**a.** Two alleles for tall stems
_____ **14.** purebred tall	**b.** One allele for tall stems and one allele for short stems
_____ **15.** hybrid tall	**c.** Two alleles for short stems

▶ Using Symbols in Genetics (pages 74–75)

16. A dominant allele is represented by a(n) _____ letter.

17. A recessive allele is represented by a(n) _____ letter.

18. How would a geneticist write the alleles to show that a tall pea plant has

one allele for tall stems and one allele for short stems? _____

▶ Mendel's Contribution (page 75)

19. Is the following sentence true or false? Some scientists during Mendel's time thought Mendel should be called the Father of Genetics.

_____

CHAPTER 3, Genetics: The Science of Heredity *(continued)*

20. Is the following sentence true or false? The importance of Mendel's work was not recognized until 34 years after he presented his results to

a scientific society. _____

📖 Reading Skill Practice

Concept maps can help you organize the terms and ideas in a chapter. Make a concept map to show the relationships among the key terms *genes, alleles, recessive alleles,* and *dominant alleles.* For more information about concept maps, see page 766 in the Skills Handbook of your textbook. Do your work on a separate sheet of paper.

SECTION 3-2 **Probability and Genetics** (pages 78-83)

This section explains what probability is and how the laws of probability can be used in the study of genetics.

▶ **Introduction** (page 78)

1. The likelihood that a particular event will occur is called

_____.

▶ **Principles of Probability** (page 79)

2. Circle the letter of each answer that equals the probability that a tossed coin will land heads up.

a. 1 in 2

b. ½

c. 50 percent

d. 20 percent

Science Explorer *Focus on Life Science*

3. Is the following sentence true or false? When you toss a coin 20 times, you will always get 10 heads and 10 tails. _____

4. If you toss a coin five times and it lands heads up each time, can you expect the coin to land heads up on the sixth toss? Explain.

_____

_____

▶ Mendel and Probability (page 80)

5. When Mendel crossed two hybrid plants for stem height (Tt), what results did he always get? _____

_____

_____

6. Mendel realized that the principles of probability could be used to _____ the results of genetic crosses.

▶ Punnett Squares (pages 80–81)

7. A chart that shows all the possible combinations of alleles that can result from a genetic cross is called a(n) _____.

8. Write in the alleles of the parents and the possible allele combinations of the offspring in the Punnett square below.

CHAPTER 3, Genetics: The Science of Heredity (continued)

9. Calculate the probability that an offspring in the Punnett square on

   page 25 will be *TT*. _____

10. In the Punnett square on page 25, what possible allele combinations

    can a tall offspring have? _____

▶ Phenotypes and Genotypes (page 82)

Match the term with its definition.

Term	Definition
_____ 11. phenotype	**a.** An organism with two identical alleles for a trait
_____ 12. genotype	**b.** An organism's physical appearance, or visible traits
_____ 13. homozygous	**c.** An organism's genetic makeup, or allele combinations
_____ 14. heterozygous	**d.** An organism that has two different alleles for a trait

15. Mendel used the term _____ to describe heterozygous
    pea plants.

▶ Codominance (pages 82–83)

16. Is the following sentence true or false? In codominance, the alleles are

    neither dominant nor recessive. _____

17. A black Erminette chicken is crossed with a white Erminette chicken.

    What color are the offspring? _____

    _____

    _____

18. In cattle, red hair and white hair are codominant. Cattle with both

    white hair and red hair are _____.

SECTION 3-3 **The Cell and Inheritance**
(pages 86-90)

This section describes how one set of chromosomes from each parent is passed on to the offspring.

▶ Chromosomes and Inheritance (page 87)

1. Circle the letter of each sentence that is true about what Sutton observed about chromosome number.

   a. Grasshopper sex cells have half the number of chromosomes as body cells.

   b. Grasshopper body cells have half the number of chromosomes as sex cells.

   c. Grasshopper body cells and sex cells have the same number of chromosomes.

   d. When grasshopper sex cells join, the fertilized egg has the same number of chromosomes as the body cells of the parents.

2. What is the chromosome theory of inheritance? _____

   _____

   _____

▶ Meiosis (pages 88–89)

3. Complete the cycle diagram, which describes the events that occur during meiosis.

Parent cell with four chromosomes are

arranged in _____ pairs.

Chromosome pairs

_____ and are

distributed to sex cells. Each sex cell has

_____ chromosomes.

Sex cells combine to produce offspring.

Each offspring has _____

chromosomes, one pair from each parent.

© Prentice-Hall, Inc.

CHAPTER 3, Genetics: The Science of Heredity *(continued)*

4. What is meiosis? _____

_____

_____

▶ Meiosis and Punnett Squares (page 88)

5. A Punnett square is a shorthand way to show the events that occur at

_____.

6. Is the following sentence true or false? When chromosome pairs separate

into different sex cells, the alleles of genes stay together. _____

7. If the male parent cell is heterozygous for a trait, *Tt*, what alleles could

the sperm cells possibly have? _____

_____

▶ Chromosomes (page 90)

8. Human body cells contain _____ pairs, or _____
chromosomes.

9. Is the following sentence true or false? Larger organisms always have
more chromosomes in their body cells than smaller organisms.

_____

10. How are the genes lined up in a pair of chromosomes? _____

_____

_____

Reading Skill Practice

The photographs and illustrations in textbooks can help you better understand what you are reading. Look at Figure 14 on page 90. Describe the idea that this figure is showing. Do your work on a separate sheet of paper.

SECTION 3-4 The DNA Connection (pages 91-96)

This section tells how the DNA molecule is related to genes, chromosomes, and the inheritance of traits.

▶ The Genetic Code (pages 91–92)

1. Circle the letter of each sentence that is true about the genes, chromosomes, and proteins.

   a. Genes control the production of proteins in an organism's cells.

   b. Proteins help determine the size, shape, and other traits of an organism.

   c. Chromosomes are made up mostly of proteins.

   d. A single gene on a chromosome contains only one pair of nitrogen bases.

2. A DNA molecule is made up of these four nitrogen bases.

   a. _____

   b. _____

   c. _____

   d. _____

3. What is the genetic code? _____

   _____

   _____

4. One group of three nitrogen bases codes for one _____.

5. What are the building blocks of proteins? _____

▶ How Cells Make Proteins (pages 92–95)

6. What happens during protein synthesis? _____

   _____

   _____

   _____

CHAPTER 3, Genetics: The Science of Heredity *(continued)*

7. Proteins are made on _____ in the cytoplasm of the cell.

8. Complete this Venn diagram to show some of the similarities and differences between DNA and RNA.

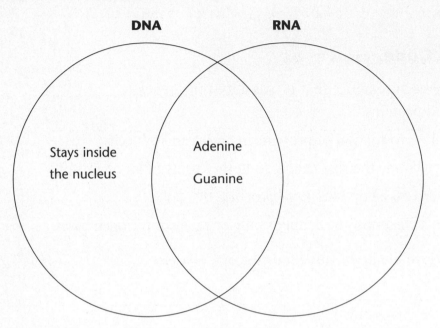

DNA   **RNA**

Stays inside
the nucleus

Adenine

Guanine

9. List the two kinds of RNA and tell their jobs.

a. _____

_____

_____

b. _____

_____

_____

10. Circle the letter of the first step in protein synthesis.

   a. Transfer RNA carries amino acids to the ribosome.

   b. The ribosome releases the completed protein chain.

   c. Messenger RNA enters the cytoplasm and attaches to a ribosome.

   d. DNA "unzips" to direct the production of a strand of messenger RNA.

11. Circle the letter of the last step in protein synthesis.

    a. Transfer RNA carries amino acids to the ribosome.

    b. The ribosome releases the completed protein chain.

    c. Messenger RNA enters the cytoplasm and attaches to a ribosome.

    d. DNA "unzips" to direct the production of a strand of messenger RNA.

▶ Mutations (pages 94–96)

12. What is a mutation? _____

_____

_____

13. How can mutations affect protein synthesis in cells? _____

_____

_____

_____

14. Circle the letter of each sentence that is true about mutations.

    a. Cells with mutations will always make normal proteins.

    b. Some mutations occur when one nitrogen base is substituted for another.

    c. Some mutations occur when chromosomes don't separate correctly during meiosis.

    d. Mutations that occur in a body cell can be passed on to an offspring.

15. Mutations can be a source of genetic _____.

16. Is the following sentence true or false? All mutations are harmful.

_____

17. Mutations that are _____ improve an organism's chances for survival and reproduction.

18. Whether a mutation is harmful or helpful depends partly on an

organism's _____.

CHAPTER 3, Genetics: The Science of Heredity (continued)

WordWise

Use the clues below to identify key terms from Chapter 3. Write the terms below, putting one letter in each blank. When you finish, the word enclosed in the diagonal lines will reveal what Mendel studied.

Clues

1. The process by which the number of chromosomes is reduced by half in sex cells

2. A chart that shows all possible allele combinations resulting from a genetic cross

3. An organism's physical appearance

4. RNA that is a copy of the DNA message that can enter the cytoplasm

5. An organism that has two different alleles for a trait

6. Likelihood that a certain event will occur

7. An allele whose trait always shows up in the organism when the allele is present

8. Physical characteristic of an organism

9. A factor that controls a trait

10. The scientific study of heredity

11. One that always produces offspring with the same form of a trait as the parent

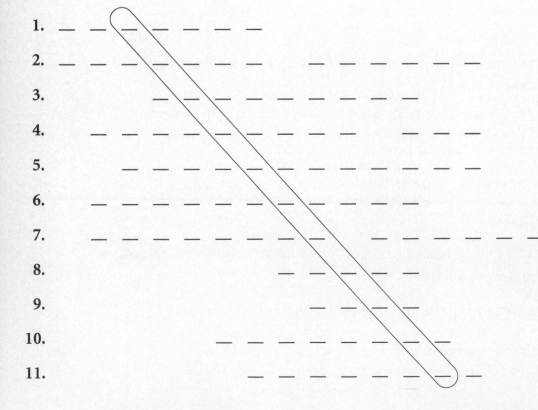

CHAPTER 4

MODERN GENETICS

••

SECTION 4-1 **Human Inheritance**
(pages 102-108)

This section tells why some traits in people have many possible phenotypes. It also describes the tools scientists use to learn how traits are inherited in families.

▶ **Traits Controlled by Single Genes** (pages 102–103)

1. The probability that two heterozygous parents for widow's peak will

   have a child with a straight hairline is _____ percent.

2. Is the following sentence true or false? Smile dimples are caused by the

   recessive allele of a gene. _____

▶ **Multiple Alleles** (page 103)

3. A gene with three or more alleles for a single trait has _____.

4. Is the following sentence true or false? Even though a gene has multiple

   alleles, a person can carry only two of those alleles. _____

5. Complete the table by writing all possible combinations of alleles for
   each blood type.

Blood Types	
Blood Type	**Combination of Alleles**
A	or
B	or
AB	
O	

CHAPTER 4, Modern Genetics *(continued)*

▶ Traits Controlled by Many Genes (page 104)

6. Why do some human traits, such as height and skin color, show a large

number of phenotypes? _____

_____

_____

7. Is the following sentence true or false? Skin color is controlled by more

than one gene. _____

▶ The Effect of Environment (page 104)

8. The effects of genes are often altered by the _____.

9. List three environmental factors that have caused people to grow taller

over time.

a. _____

b. _____

c. _____

▶ Male or Female? (page 105)

10. Is the following sentence true or false? Genes on chromosomes

determine whether a baby is a boy or a girl. _____

11. Females have two _____ chromosomes. Males have one

_____ chromosome and one _____ chromosome.

12. Circle the letter of each sentence that is true about the sex
chromosomes.

a. All eggs have one X chromosome.

b. Half of a male's sperm cells have an X chromosome.

c. None of a male's sperm cells have a Y chromosome.

d. The egg determines the sex of the child.

▶ Sex-Linked Genes (pages 106–107)

13. Genes on the X and Y chromosomes are called _____.

14. Why are males more likely than females to have a sex-linked trait that is

    recessive? _____

15. Is the following question true or false? A carrier for colorblindness is

    colorblind. _____

16. Why is a son who receives the allele for colorblindness from his mother

    always going to be colorblind? _____

    _____

    _____

▶ Pedigrees (pages 107–108)

17. A chart or "family tree" that tracks which members of a family have a

    certain trait is called a(n) _____.

18. Is the following sentence true or false? On a pedigree, a circle represents

    a male. _____

- -

SECTION 4-2 Human Genetic Disorders (pages 109-113)

This section describes how changes in the DNA of some genes have affected certain traits in humans.

▶ Introduction (page 109)

1. An abnormal condition that a person inherits through genes or

   chromosomes is called a(n) _____.

2. What causes genetic disorders? _____

   _____

CHAPTER 4, Modern Genetics *(continued)*

▶ **Cystic Fibrosis** (page 110)

3. What is cystic fibrosis? _____

_____

_____

4. Is the following sentence true or false? Cystic fibrosis is caused by a

mutation that is the dominant allele of a gene. _____

▶ **Sickle-Cell Disease** (pages 110–111)

5. Circle the protein that is not normal in people with sickle-cell disease.

   a. mucus   **b.** hemoglobin

   c. red blood cells   **d.** clotting protein

6. The allele for the sickle-cell trait is _____ with the
   normal allele.

▶ **Hemophilia** (page 111)

7. Is the following sentence true or false? Hemophilia is caused by a

   dominant allele on the X chromosome. _____

8. Hemophilia occurs more often in _____.

9. How is hemophilia treated? _____

_____

_____

▶ **Down Syndrome** (page 112)

10. Circle the letter of the cause of Down syndrome.

   a. recessive allele   **b.** dominant allele

   c. too many chromosomes   **d.** too few chromosomes

11. Down syndrome most often occurs when _____ fail to
    separate properly during meiosis.

▶ **Diagnosing Genetic Disorders** (pages 112–113)

12. Complete the concept map to show some tools used by doctors to detect genetic disorders.

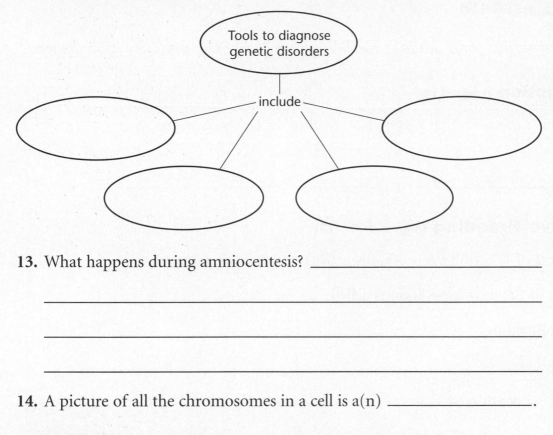

13. What happens during amniocentesis? _____

_____

_____

_____

14. A picture of all the chromosomes in a cell is a(n) _____.

▶ **Genetic Counseling** (page 113)

15. How do genetic counselors help couples? _____

_____

_____

![book icon] **Reading Skill Practice**

A compare/contrast table organizes information that you have read. Make a table to compare and contrast the four genetic disorders described in Section 4–2. The column headings should be the names of the genetic disorders. The row headings should include descriptions and causes of the disorders. For more information about compare/contrast tables, see page 766 in the Skills Handbook of your textbook. Do your work on a separate sheet of paper.

CHAPTER 4, Modern Genetics *(continued)*

· ·

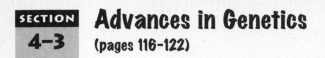

SECTION 4–3 **Advances in Genetics**
(pages 116-122)

This section describes some of the research in genetic technology and how it can be used.

▶ **Introduction** (page 116)

1. List the three methods that people have used to develop organisms with desirable traits.

   a. _____ b. _____ c. _____

▶ **Selective Breeding** (pages 116–117)

2. The process of selecting a few organisms with the desired traits to serve

   as parents of the next generation is called _____.

3. What is inbreeding? _____

   _____

4. Is the following sentence true or false? In hybridization, breeders cross

   two individuals that are genetically identical. _____

5. What is commonly produced today by hybridization? _____

   _____

▶ **Cloning** (page 118)

6. Circle the letter of each sentence that is true about cloning.

   a. A clone has exactly the same genes as the organism from which it was
   produced.

   b. A cutting is one way to make a clone of an animal.

   c. It's easier to clone an animal than it is to clone a plant.

   d. Dolly, the lamb, was the first clone of an adult mammal ever produced.

7. Is the following sentence true or false? Cloning can be done only in

   animals. _____

► Genetic Engineering (pages 118–121)

8. In genetic engineering, genes from one organism are transferred into

the _____ of another organism.

9. Complete this flowchart about genetic engineering in bacteria.

Genetic Engineering in Bacteria

Human DNA is spliced into the _____,
which is a small ring of DNA in bacteria.

↓

The _____ takes up the plasmid. It
now contains the human gene.

↓

The bacterial cell produces the _____
that the human gene codes for.

10. What is gene therapy? _____

_____

_____

► DNA Fingerprinting (page 121)

11. How are DNA samples similar to fingerprints? _____

_____

_____

12. DNA fingerprinting is being used to help solve _____.

► The Human Genome Project (page 122)

13. All the DNA in one cell of an organism is a(n) _____.

14. What is the goal of the Human Genome Project? _____

_____

CHAPTER 4, **Modern Genetics** (continued)

WordWise

Use the clues to identify key terms from Chapter 4. Write the terms on the lines. Then find the words hidden in the puzzle and circle them. Words are across or up-and-down.

Clues	Key Terms
A procedure in which fluid surrounding a developing baby is removed	_____
A person with one recessive and one dominant allele for a trait	_____
An organism that is genetically identical to the organism from which it was produced	_____
All the DNA in one cell of an organism	_____
Breeders cross two genetically different organisms	_____
Breeders cross two genetically identical organisms	_____
A picture of all the chromosomes in a cell	_____
A chart that tracks which family member has a certain trait	_____

```
h k c i p a e g h r y x i n b r e e d i n g
k a e r g e n i e m i b h n c e t a c k h p
a r h y b r i d i z a t i o n b w s a t r e
d y o d i c i j a t w e g l h a g e r s c d
g o n k a l r e n t l d a l a m e i r d s i
o t e a p o d i w t k s a e r p n f i m c g
r y k r g n n i r i h r e w x p o n e s s r
h p l y p e l a g v p h y b s z m a r e w e
n e e a m n i o c e n t e s i s e k p y r e
```

EVOLUTION

....

SECTION 5-1 **Darwin's Voyage**
(pages 136-146)

This section discusses Charles Darwin and his theories of evolution, which are based on what he saw during his trip around the world.

▶ Darwin's Observations (page 137)

1. Is the following sentence true or false? Charles Darwin was not surprised by the variety of living things he saw on his voyage around the world.

   _____

2. A group of similar organisms that can mate with each other and

   produce fertile offspring is called a(n) _____.

3. Is the following sentence true or false? Darwin observed the greatest

   diversity of organisms on the Galapagos Islands. _____

▶ Similarities and Differences (page 138)

4. Circle the letter of each sentence that is true about Darwin's observations.

   a. Many Galapagos organisms were similar to organisms on mainland South America.

   b. Iguanas on the Galapagos Islands had small claws for climbing trees.

   c. Darwin thought Galapagos animals and plants came from mainland South America.

   d. All tortoises living in the Galapagos Islands looked exactly the same.

5. Darwin noticed many differences among similar _____ as he traveled from one Galapagos island to the next.

CHAPTER 5, Evolution *(continued)*

▶ Adaptations (page 139)

Look at the bird beaks below. Match the bird beaks with the kind of food the bird eats.

Kind of Food   **Bird Beaks**

_____ **6.** insects

_____ **7.** seeds

a.   b.

8. A trait that helps an organism survive and reproduce is a(n)

_____.

▶ Evolution (pages 139–140)

9. Circle the letter of each sentence that is true about Darwin's conclusions.

a. Darwin understood immediately why Galapagos organisms had many different adaptations.

b. Darwin thought that Galapagos organisms gradually changed over many generations.

c. Darwin believed that evolution had occurred on the Galapagos Islands.

d. Darwin knew how certain traits were selected for in nature.

10. Circle the letter of a well-tested concept that explains many observations.

a. idea   **b.** evolution   **c.** scientific theory   **d.** hypothesis

▶ Natural Selection (pages 140–141)

11. In his book, *The Origin of Species*, Darwin explained that evolution

occurs by means of _____.

12. Is the following sentence true or false? Individuals with variations that make them better adapted to their environment will not survive.

_____

© Prentice-Hall, Inc.

Match the factors that affect the process of natural selection with their definitions.

Definitions	Factors
_____ 13. Caused by limited food and other resources	a. overproduction
_____ 14. Differences between individuals of the same species	b. competition
_____ 15. Species produce more offspring than can survive.	c. variations

▶ The Role of Genes in Evolution (page 144)

16. Is the following sentence true or false? Only traits that are controlled by

genes can be acted upon by natural selection. _____

17. Is the following sentence true or false? Darwin knew all about genes

and mutations. _____

▶ Evolution in Action (page 144)

18. During a drought on one of the Galapagos Islands in 1977, only finches

with _____ and _____ beaks were better
able to survive.

19. Is the following sentence true or false? Evolution by natural selection

can occur in as short a time as one year. _____

▶ How Do New Species Form? (page 145)

20. When does a new species form? _____

_____

_____

21. Give an example of how a group can be separated from the rest of its

species. _____

_____

CHAPTER 5, Evolution (continued)

▶ Continental Drift (page 146)

22. Pangaea gradually split apart in a process called _____.

23. What happened to plant and animal species during continental drift?

_____

_____

_____

Reading Skill Practice

The glossary on pages 776–787 of your textbook gives the definitions of all the key terms. You can use the glossary when you need to find the meaning of a key term. Find and write the definitions of the terms *adaptation, evolution, natural selection,* and *variation.* Do your work on a separate sheet of paper.

SECTION 5-2 The Fossil Record (pages 147-150)

This section explains what fossils are and how fossils give clues about evolution.

▶ What Is a Fossil? (page 147)

1. Some of the most important clues to Earth's past are _____.

2. Is the following sentence true or false? Only the soft parts of an animal

   remain to form a fossil. _____

3. In what conditions do most fossils form? _____

_____

_____

_____

Science Explorer *Focus on Life Science*

▶ What Do Fossils Reveal? (page 148)

4. The millions of fossils that scientists have collected are called the

_____.

5. Is the following sentence true or false? The remains of all organisms have

become fossils. _____

6. How have scientists learned about extinct species? _____

_____

7. According to the fossil record, fish evolved about _____ years

ago. The first land plants evolved about _____ years ago.

▶ How Fast Does Evolution Occur? (pages 148–150)

8. Complete the table below about the two theories of evolution.

How Fast Does Evolution Occur?		
Theory of Evolution	**What the Theory Says**	**Intermediate Forms of Species?**
Gradualism		
Punctuated Equilibria		

📖 Reading Skill Practice

Outlines are useful tools to help you organize and remember what you have read. In outlines, the major headings of a section are listed in order. Under each heading, one or two important ideas about that topic are listed. Write an outline of the subsection, *How Fast Does Evolution Occur?* Do your work on a separate sheet of paper.

CHAPTER 5, Evolution *(continued)*

SECTION 5-3 Other Evidence for Evolution
(pages 151-155)

This section tells how scientists decide which living things are related.

▶ **Introduction** (page 151)

1. Complete the concept map to show what kinds of evidence scientists use to decide whether or not organisms are related.

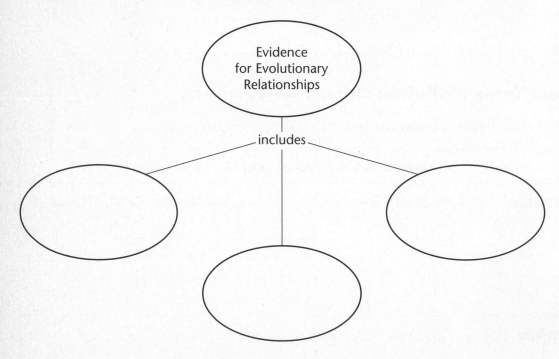

Evidence for Evolutionary Relationships

includes

▶ **Similarities in Body Structure** (pages 151–152)

2. Why do scientists classify fish, amphibians, reptiles, birds, and mammals

together in one group? _____

_____

_____

_____

3. Similar body structures that related species have inherited from a

common ancestor are called _____ .

Science Explorer *Focus on Life Science*

▶ Similarities in Early Development (pages 152–153)

4. What similarities in development lead scientists to infer that turtles, chickens, and rats share a common ancestor? _____

_____

_____

5. Evidence supports the conclusion that turtles are more closely related to _____ than they are to _____.

▶ Similarities in DNA (pages 153–154)

6. Is the following sentence true or false? The more closely related species are, the more similar their DNA sequences. _____

7. What have scientists learned about the elephant shrew based on DNA evidence? _____

_____

_____

8. The DNA from _____ is providing scientists with new evidence about evolution.

▶ Combining the Evidence (pages 154–155)

9. Circle the letter of each sentence that is true about evolutionary relationships of organisms.

   a. DNA comparisons show that dogs are more similar to coyotes than to wolves.

   b. Scientists had already made good conclusions about the evolutionary relationships of dogs, wolves, and coyotes based on their similar structures and development.

   c. A branching tree shows how scientists think different groups of organisms are related.

   d. DNA evidence shows that giant pandas are more closely related to raccoons than to bears.

CHAPTER 5, Evolution *(continued)*

WordWise

Answer the clues to solve this crossword puzzle.

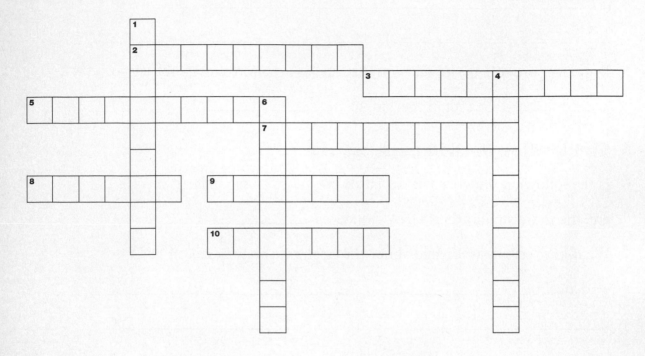

Clues down

1. The gradual change in a species over time

4. A trait that helps an organism survive and reproduce

6. The process by which individuals that are better adapted to their environment are more likely to survive is called natural ____.

Clues across

2. Any difference between individuals of the same species

3. The theory that evolution occurs slowly but steadily

5. Similar structures that related species inherited from a common ancestor are ____ structures.

7. The theory that evolution occurs during short periods of rapid change is punctuated _____.

8. The preserved remains of an organism

9. A group of similar organisms that can mate and produce fertile offspring

10. No members of a species are still alive

CHAPTER 6

EARTH'S HISTORY

Fossils
(pages 162-168)

This section explains what fossils are and how they form.

▶ **Earth's Rocks and the Rock Cycle** (pages 162–163)

Match the term with its definition.

Term	Definition
_____ **1.** rocks	**a.** Forms when an existing rock is changed by heat, pressure, or chemical reactions
_____ **2.** igneous rock	**b.** Forms when molten material cools and hardens below or on Earth's surface
_____ **3.** sedimentary rock	
_____ **4.** metamorphic rock	**c.** Made of mixtures of minerals and other materials
	d. Forms when particles of other rocks or the remains of plants and animals are pressed and cemented together

5. The rock cycle is caused by _____ inside Earth and at Earth's surface.

6. Circle the letter of each sentence that is true about the rock cycle.

   a. The rock cycle occurs only beneath Earth's surface.

   b. During the rock cycle, rocks slowly change from one kind to another.

   c. The rock cycle can follow many different pathways.

   d. Metamorphic rock ends the rock cycle.

7. Is the following sentence true or false? Rock pushed beneath Earth's

   surface is melted by the heat of Earth's interior. _____

CHAPTER 6, Earth's History *(continued)*

8. Draw arrows on the diagram below to complete the rock cycle.

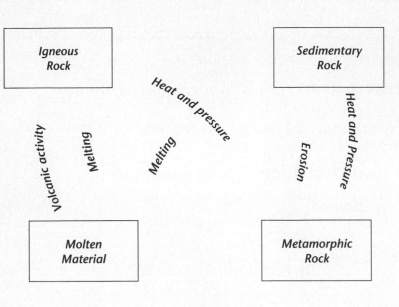

▶ Evidence of Ancient Life (page 164)

9. Is the following sentence true or false? Fossils are usually found in

igneous rock. _____

10. List three things that paleontologists learn by studying fossils.

a. _____

b. _____

c. _____

▶ Kinds of Fossils (pages 164–167)

11. Is the following sentence true or false? Fossils can form when the

remains of an organism decay. _____

12. Fossils in which minerals replace all or part of an organism are called

_____ fossils.

13. Is the following sentence true or false? Petrified fossils can form when the minerals in water make a copy of the organism. _____

14. Circle the letter of each sentence that is true about molds and casts.

    a. Molds and casts both copy the shape of ancient organisms.

    b. A mold forms when the hard part of an organism is buried in sediment.

    c. A cast is a hollow area in sediment in the shape of an organism.

    d. Molds and casts do not show details of the organism's structure.

15. What is a carbon film? _____

_____

_____

16. Is the following sentence true or false? A carbon film forms when minerals preserve the delicate parts of an organism. _____

17. Circle the letter of each trace fossil.

    a. footprints   **b.** animal trails   **c.** animal shells   **d.** burrows

18. What can a paleontologist infer by looking at fossil footprints?

_____

_____

_____

_____

19. What are three ways that the remains of organisms have been preserved?

    a. _____

    b. _____

    c. _____

▶ Fossils and Past Environments (page 168)

20. Is the following sentence true or false? It is very difficult for scientists to learn about Earth's past environments by studying fossils. _____

CHAPTER 6, **Earth's History** (*continued*)

21. Circle the letter before the environment where coal can form.

    a. warm, shallow seas   **b.** cold, icy regions

    c. warm, swampy regions   **d.** cold ocean bottoms

Reading Skill Practice

Flowcharts and diagrams are both useful tools to help you organize the steps in a process. Look carefully at the diagram in Figure 3 on page 164. Use the diagram to help you make a flowchart that shows the steps of fossil formation. For more information about flowcharts, see page 767 in the Skills Handbook of your textbook. Do your work on a separate sheet of paper.

SECTION 6–2   **Finding the Relative Age of Rocks**
(pages 169-173)

This section tells how scientists determine how old rocks are.

▶ **Relative and Absolute Ages** (page 169)

Match the term with its definition.

Term	Definition
_____ **1.** relative age	**a.** The number of years since the rock formed
_____ **2.** absolute age	**b.** The age of a rock compared to the ages of other rocks

▶ **The Position of Rock Layers** (page 170)

3. According to the law of superposition, the _____ layer is

    at the bottom. Each higher layer is _____ than the layers below it.

4. Is the following sentence true or false? The deeper one travels into the

    Grand Canyon, the younger the rocks become. _____

▶ Other Clues to Relative Age (page 171)

5. Complete the table below about the clues that geologists use to find the relative ages of rocks.

Clues to the Relative Ages of Rocks		
Clues	**How It Forms**	**What Clues Tell Geologists**
Extrusion		
Intrusion		
Fault		

▶ Gaps in the Geologic Record (page 172)

6. What is an unconformity? _____

_____

_____

7. Look carefully at Figure 13 on page 172. Then describe how an

unconformity can form. _____

_____

_____

_____

_____

▶ Using Fossils to Date Rocks (pages 172–173)

8. Geologists use _____ fossils to match rock layers in different locations.

CHAPTER 6, Earth's History (continued)

9. Circle the letter of each sentence that is true about index fossils.

   a. Index fossils must be found in many different areas.

   b. Index fossils must represent an organism that lived for a very long time.

   c. Index fossils tell the absolute ages of the rock layers in which they occur.

   d. A type of trilobite that is different from other trilobites is a useful index fossil.

Reading Skill Practice

Taking notes as you read can help you remember what you have read. Reread Section 6–2. As you read it, make a list of the different ways that geologists can find the relative age of rocks. Give one or two details about each method that you list. Do your work on a separate sheet of paper.

SECTION 6-3 **Radioactive Dating** (pages 175-178)

This section describes how scientists find out when rocks formed.

▶ Changing From One Element to Another (pages 175–176)

1. A type of matter in which all the atoms making up the matter are the

   same is called a(n) _____.

2. Is the following sentence true or false? All elements will decay over time.

   _____

3. What occurs during radioactive decay? _____

   _____

   _____

   _____

4. Circle the letter of the kind of rock in which radioactive elements occur naturally.

a. sedimentary   **b.** igneous   **c.** metamorphic   **d.** fossil

5. How do scientists use the rate at which radioactive elements decay in rocks?

_____

_____

▶ The Rate of Radioactive Decay (page 176)

6. Circle the letter before each sentence that is true about radioactive decay.

   a. Over time, the amount of a radioactive element in igneous rock will go up.

   b. The rate of decay of each radioactive element is always changing.

   c. The rate of radioactive decay is an element's half-life.

   d. The half-life of a radioactive element is the time it takes for half of the radioactive atoms to decay.

7. Look at the radioactive elements listed in Figure 18 on page 176. Which element has the longest half-life? _____ Which element has the shortest half-life? _____

▶ Absolute Ages From Radioactive Dating (pages 176–177)

8. Is the following sentence true or false? Geologists use radioactive dating to find the absolute ages of rocks. _____

9. What two things must scientists measure to find the age of a rock?

   a. _____

_____

   b. _____

_____

10. Is the following sentence true or false? By calculating the ratio of the radioactive element to the stable element, scientists can determine the age of a rock. _____

CHAPTER 6, Earth's History *(continued)*

11. Complete the table to compare two different types of radioactive dating.

Elements Used in Radioactive Dating		
Elements	**Decays To**	**Used For Dating**
Potassium-40		
Carbon-14		

12. Is the following sentence true or false? Carbon-14 can date materials

that are billions of years old because it has a long half-life. _____

▶ Radioactive Dating of Rock Layers (page 178)

13. Is the following sentence true or false? Radioactive dating can be used

only for igneous rocks. _____

14. Why can't radioactive dating be used to date sedimentary rocks?

_____

_____

_____

15. What do scientists use igneous intrusions and extrusions for?

_____

_____

▶ How Old Is Earth? (page 178)

16. Circle the letter of each sentence that is true about Earth's age.

    a. The oldest rocks ever found on Earth are about 4.0 billion years old.

    b. The moon is about the same age as Earth.

    c. Earth formed from materials that came from the moon.

    d. Scientists don't know how old moon rocks are.

17. Scientists infer that Earth is roughly _____ years old.

Science Explorer *Focus on Life Science*

SECTION 6-4 The Geologic Time Scale (pages 179-181)

This section tells what the geologic time scale is and how it is used to show Earth's history.

▶ **Introduction** (page 179)

1. Complete the diagram below by writing the events that occurred at that time.

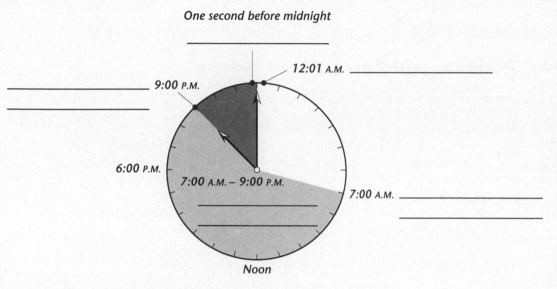

▶ **The Geologic Time Scale** (page 179)

2. Is the following sentence true or false? Using months, years, and centuries is a very useful way of thinking about Earth's long history. _____

3. What is the geologic time scale? _____

_____

_____

4. The divisions of the geologic time scale depend on events in the history

of _____ on Earth.

▶ **Divisions of Geologic Time** (page 180)

5. Geologic time begins with a long span of time called _____.

CHAPTER 6, Earth's History *(continued)*

6. Complete this concept map to show the three basic units of the geologic time scale.

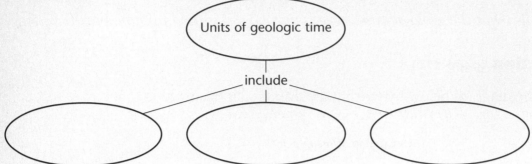

▶ **Eras, Periods, and Epochs** (pages 180–181)

Match each unit of time with its characteristics.

Unit of Time	Characteristics
_____ **7.** Paleozoic Era	**a.** Part of the Mesozoic Era; named for the Jura Mountains in France
_____ **8.** Mesozoic Era	
_____ **9.** Cenozoic Era	**b.** Most animals in this era were invertebrates
_____ **10.** Jurassic Period	**c.** Earth's most recent era
_____ **11.** Carboniferous Period	**d.** Subdivisions of time in the periods of the Cenozoic Era
_____ **12.** epochs	**e.** Part of the Paleozoic Era; named for large coal deposits that formed then
	f. The middle era; the Age of Dinosaurs

SECTION 6-5 **A Trip Through Geologic Time** (pages 184-196)

This section describes the major events in Earth's geologic history and in the development of living things on Earth.

▶ **Precambrian Time** (pages 184–185)

1. What did Earth form from? _____

_____

2. Is the following sentence true or false? Scientists know exactly when life

began on Earth. _____

3. Circle the letter of the present-day organism that the earliest life forms
were probably most similar to.

    a. bacteria   **b.** plants   **c.** sponges   **d.** worms

4. Is the following sentence true or false? The amount of oxygen in the
atmosphere increased as organisms began making food using energy

from the sun. _____

5. Why did the sponges and worms from Precambrian time leave few fossils?

_____

▶ **The Paleozoic Era** (pages 185–191)

6. What happened during the Cambrian Explosion? _____

_____

7. Complete this flowchart to show what living things evolved during the
Paleozoic Era.

The Paleozoic Era

During the Silurian Period, simple _____ began to
grow on land in damp areas.

↓

During the Devonian Period, animals that live part of their life on land
and part of their life in water, or _____, evolved.

↓

During the Carboniferous Period, _____ that have
scaly skin and lay eggs with tough, leathery shells first developed.

↓

At the end of the Paleozoic Era, a(n) _____ occurred
in which many types of living things died out at the same time.

CHAPTER 6, Earth's History (continued)

8. Is the following sentence true or false? During the Cambrian Period, all

    animals lived in the sea. _____

9. An animal with a backbone is called a(n) _____.

10. What were the first vertebrates to evolve? _____

    _____

11. What is a mass extinction? _____

    _____

▶ The Supercontinent Pangaea (page 192)

12. What is one theory for the mass extinction at the end of the Paleozoic Era?

    _____

    _____

13. What happened to Earth's continents during the Permian Period?

    _____

    _____

    _____

14. Is the following sentence true or false? The formation of Pangaea

    caused the climate on Earth to change. _____

▶ The Mesozoic Era (pages 192–195)

15. Circle the letter of the living thing that was most successful during the
    Mesozoic Era.

    a. insects   b. conifers

    c. fish   d. reptiles

16. The first warm-blooded vertebrates that feed their young milk, called

    _____, appeared during the Triassic Period.

17. The first birds appeared in the _____ Period of the Mesozoic Era.

18. Circle the letter of each sentence that is true about living things in the Cretaceous Period.

    a. Mammals continued evolving, even though dinosaurs dominated the land.

    b. Flying reptiles were better adapted to flying than birds.

    c. Turtles and crocodiles became extinct.

    d. Flowering plants began to evolve.

19. What is one hypothesis for the mass extinction at the end of the

Cretaceous Period? _____

_____

_____

_____

▶ **The Cenozoic Era** (pages 195–196)

20. Why didn't mammals evolve more during the Mesozoic Era?

_____

_____

_____

21. Is the following sentence true or false? Mollusks, whales, and dolphins

are all mammals that evolved in the oceans. _____

22. How did Earth's climate change in the Quaternary Period? _____

_____

_____

23. Human ancestors first appeared in the _____ Period.

CHAPTER 6, Earth's History (continued)

WordWise

Use the clues to fill in the key terms. Then transfer each letter to the correspondingly numbered square below. The hidden message will be a concept from Chapter 6.

Clues   **Terms**

A gap in the geologic record

— — — — — — — — — — —
1 2 3 4   5 6 7 8 9 10

Rock that forms from molten
material

— — — — — — — — — —
11 12 13 14 15 16 17

An animal that lives part of
its life in water and part of
its life on land

— — — — — — — —
18 19 20   21

A copy of an ancient
organism's shape

— — — —
22 23

Lava that hardens on Earth's
surface

— — — — — — — —
24   25   26 27

A series of processes that slowly
change rocks from one kind
to another

— — — — — — — — —
28 29   30   31

A scientist who studies fossils

— — — — — — — — — — — —
32   33   34   35   36   37 38

Tiny particles that make up
all matter

— — — — —
39 40   41

Animals with a backbone

— — — — — — — — —
42 43 44 45   46 47 48 49

The time it takes for half of
a radioactive element to decay

— — — — – — — —
50   51   52

Units of time that further
divide periods

— — — — —
53 54 55

Hidden Message

— — — — — — — — — —   — — —   — — —   — — — — — — — — — —
41 17 51 45 2 34 21 55 9 15   1 49 24   40 20 52   12 31 4 32 53 36 27 3

— — — —   — — — — —   — —   — — — — — — — —
44 11 7 48   26 29 18 35 42   47 14   19 33 28 25 43 39 10

— — — — —   —   — — — — — — .
13 46 6 38 54   22   50 8 37 23 5 16 30

CHAPTER 7

LIVING THINGS

· ·

SECTION 7–1 **What Is Life?**
(pages 206–213)

This section explains the characteristics of living things and what living things need to survive.

▶ **The Characteristics of Living Things** (pages 206–209)

1. What is an organism? _____

_____

2. List six characteristics that all living things share.

    a. _____   b. _____

    c. _____   d. _____

    e. _____   f. _____

3. The basic building blocks of all organisms are _____.

4. Is the following sentence true or false? Most cells can be seen only with a

    microscope, a tool that magnifies small objects. _____

5. Is the following sentence true or false? An organism made of many cells

    is a unicellular organism. _____

6. Circle the letter of the most abundant chemical in cells.
    a. proteins   **b.** carbohydrates   **c.** water   **d.** nucleic acids

7. Lipids and _____ are the building materials of cells.

8. Is the following sentence true or false? The cells of organisms use energy

    for growth and repair. _____

CHAPTER 7, Living Things *(continued)*

9. What is development? _____

_____

_____

10. Circle the letter of a change in an organism's surroundings that causes the organism to react.

    a. growth   **b.** response   **c.** stimulus   **d.** development

11. Give one example of a stimulus and one example of a response.

    Stimulus: _____

    Response: _____

12. All organisms can _____, or produce offspring that are similar to the parents.

▶ **Life Comes From Life** (pages 209–211)

13. Is the following sentence true or false? Frogs can sprout from mud in

    ponds. _____

14. The idea that living things can come from nonliving sources is called

    _____ .

15. What did Francesco Redi show in his experiment? _____

_____

16. The factor that a scientist changes in a controlled experiment is the

    _____ .

17. Look carefully at Exploring the *Experiments of Redi and Pasteur* on pages 210–211. Circle the letter of the variable in Redi's experiment.

    a. meat   **b.** jars   **c.** cloth   **d.** flies

18. Is the following sentence true or false? Louis Pasteur used a controlled experiment to show that bacteria arise from spontaneous generation.

    _____

▶ The Needs of Living Things (pages 210–213)

19. Complete this concept map to show what living things need to survive.

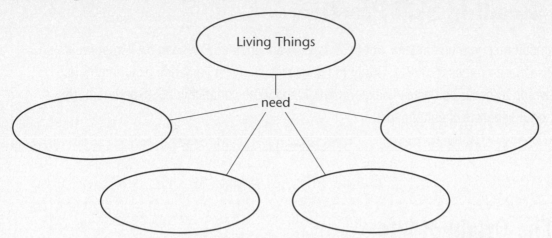

20. Is the following sentence true or false? Living things use food as their

    energy source to carry out their life functions. _____

21. Organisms that make their own food are called _____.
    Organisms that cannot make their own food are called

    _____.

22. Is the following sentence true or false? Living things can live without

    water for long periods of time. _____

23. What property of water makes it vital to living things? _____

    _____

    _____

24. Is the following sentence true or false? Organisms must compete with

    each other for space to live. _____

25. Why must living things have homeostasis, or stable internal conditions?

    _____

    _____

    _____

CHAPTER 7, Living Things *(continued)*

Reading Skill Practice

Illustrations can help you understand what you have read. Look at *Exploring the Experiments of Redi and Pasteur* on pages 210–211. Study the diagrams showing Pasteur's experiment. Use your own words to describe Pasteur's experiment. Identify the variable in his experiment. Do your work on a separate sheet of paper.

SECTION 7-2 **The Origin of Life**
(pages 215-217)

This section describes how Earth's atmosphere formed and how scientists think life first appeared on Earth.

▶ **Earth's Early Atmosphere** (pages 215–216)

1. Complete this Venn diagram to compare the major gases that made up Earth's early atmosphere and Earth's atmosphere today.

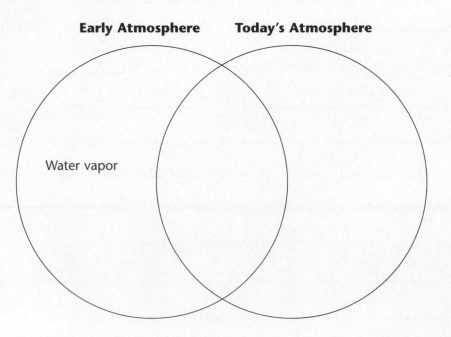

Early Atmosphere   Today's Atmosphere

Water vapor

Science Explorer *Focus on Life Science*

2. Circle the letter of each sentence that is true about the characteristics of Earth's early life forms.

   a. Early life forms needed oxygen to survive.

   b. Early life forms were probably unicellular.

   c. The first life forms probably lived in the oceans.

   d. The first organisms were very different from bacteria that live today in extreme conditions.

▶ Life's Chemicals (page 216)

3. Is the following sentence true or false? Scientists think that the first life forms on Earth probably did arise from nonliving materials.

   _____

4. What materials did Harold Urey and Stanley Miller use to recreate the

   conditions of early Earth in their laboratory? _____

   _____

   _____

5. Urey and Miller used an electric current in their experiment to simulate

   _____.

6. What were the results of Urey and Miller's experiment? _____

   _____

   _____

   _____

▶ The First Cells (page 217)

7. Scientists think that the small chemical units of life formed gradually

   over millions of years in Earth's _____.

8. Traces of ancient organisms that have been preserved in rock or other

   substances are _____.

CHAPTER 7, Living Things *(continued)*

9. Circle the letter before each sentence that is true about how life formed on Earth.

   a. Fossils show that bacteria-like living things were on Earth between 3.4 and 3.5 billion years ago.

   b. The first cells probably used the chemicals in their surroundings for energy.

   c. Cells that made their own food produced oxygen as a waste product, which built up in Earth's atmosphere.

   d. Scientists know for certain how life first appeared on Earth.

Reading Skill Practice

A flowchart is useful in organizing the sequence of events in a process. Make a flowchart to show the sequence of events that scientists hypothesize occurred in the origin of life on Earth. For more information about flowcharts, see page 767 in the Skills Handbook of your textbook. Do your work on a separate sheet of paper.

Classifying Organisms
(pages 218-227)

This section tells how scientists divide living things into groups. It also describes the first classification systems and how the theory of evolution changed classification systems.

▶ Why Do Scientists Classify? (pages 218–219)

1. The process of grouping things based on their similarities is

   _____.

2. Why do biologists use classification? _____

   _____

   _____

3. The scientific study of how living things are classified is called

   _____.

4. Is the following sentence true or false? Once an organism is classified, a

   scientist knows a lot about that organism. _____

5. Is the following sentence true or false? Biologists are the only scientists

   to classify things. _____

▶ Early Classification Systems (page 219)

6. Into what three groups did Aristotle divide animals? _____

   _____

   _____

7. Circle the letter of each sentence that is true about classification systems.

   a. Aristotle did not use his observations to group animals.

   b. Aristotle divided each group of animals into subgroups.

   c. Scientists today divide groups of animals into smaller groups based
   on their similarities.

   d. Scientists today classify animals by how they move and where they live.

▶ The Classification System of Linnaeus (pages 220–221)

8. Is the following sentence true or false? Linnaeus placed organisms into

   groups based on their features that he could observe. _____

9. In Linnaeus's naming system, called _____, each
   organism is given a two-part name.

10. Is the following sentence true or false? A species is a classification
    grouping that contains similar, closely related organisms.

    _____

11. In the scientific name for mountain lions, *Felis concolor*, which is the
    genus name and which is the species name?

    Genus: _____   Species: _____

CHAPTER 7, Living Things *(continued)*

12. Circle the letter of each sentence that is true about binomial nomenclature.

   a. A genus and a species name together identify a group of organisms.

   b. Genus and species names are in Latin because Latin was the language of scientists during Linnaeus's time.

   c. The genus name begins with a small letter.

   d. Binomial nomenclature makes it easy for scientists to talk about an organism.

▶ **Levels of Classification** (pages 222–223)

13. List the seven levels of classification used by modern biologists in order from the broadest level to the most specific level. _____

_____

_____

14. Is the following sentence true or false? The more classification levels that two organisms share, the more characteristics they have in common. _____

15. Look carefully at Figure 12 on page 223. What order does the great horned owl belong to? _____

_____

▶ **Evolution and Classification** (page 224)

16. Is the following sentence true or false? Darwin's theory of evolution did not affect the way in which species were classified. _____

17. What is evolution? _____

_____

_____

▶ Classification Today (pages 224–226)

18. Is the following sentence true or false? Species with shared ancestors are

classified more closely together. _____

19. Complete the concept map below to show four different ways scientists
get information about the evolutionary history of a species.

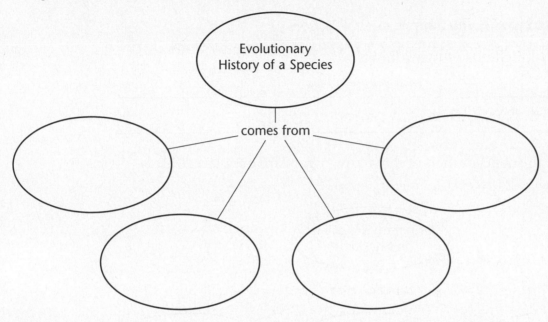

20. What do scientists today rely on primarily to determine evolutionary

history? _____

_____

▶ Using the Classification System (pages 226–227)

21. Name two ways to learn the identity of an organism.

   a. _____

   b. _____

22. Is the following sentence true or false? A taxonomic key is a book with
illustrations that highlight the differences between organisms that look

similar. _____

23. Look at the taxonomic key in Figure 16 on page 227. How many legs

does a tick have? _____

CHAPTER 7, Living Things *(continued)*

SECTION 7-4 **The Six Kingdoms** (pages 230-232)

This section describes each of the six kingdoms into which all living things are grouped.

▶ **Introduction** (page 230)

1. List the six kingdoms of living things.

   a. _____ b. _____ c. _____

   d. _____ e. _____ f. _____

2. Complete the concept map to show how organisms are placed into kingdoms.

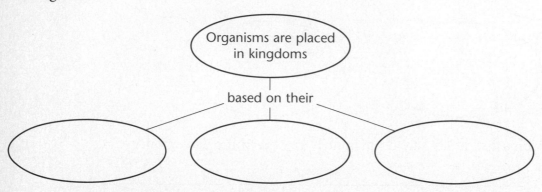

Organisms are placed in kingdoms

based on their

▶ **Archaebacteria** (pages 230–231)

3. Circle the letter of each sentence that is true about archaebacteria.

   a. Archaebacteria can be autotrophic, or able to make their own food.

   b. Archaebacteria are prokaryotes.

   c. Archaebacteria have a cell nucleus.

   d. Archaebacteria do not have nucleic acids.

4. A dense area in a cell that contains nucleic acids is a(n) _____.

▶ **Eubacteria** (page 231)

5. Is the following sentence true or false? Eubacteria have a similar

   chemical makeup to archaebacteria. _____

Science Explorer Focus on Life Science

6. What are three helpful things that eubacteria do? _____

_____

_____

_____

▶ Protists (page 231)

7. Is the following sentence true or false? Protists can be either unicellular

or multicellular. _____

8. How do protists differ from archaebacteria and eubacteria? _____

_____

_____

▶ Fungi (page 232)

9. Is the following sentence true or false? Mushrooms, molds, mildew, and

yeast are all fungi. _____

10. Circle the letter of each characteristic of fungi.

    a. eukaryotes   **b.** prokaryotes   **c.** autotrophs   **d.** heterotrophs

▶ Plants (page 232)

11. Plants are _____; they can make their own food.

12. Is the following true or false? Life on Earth could exist without plants.

_____

▶ Animals (page 232)

13. Circle the letter of each characteristic of animals.

    a. unicellular   **b.** heterotrophs   **c.** eukaryotes   **d.** autotrophs

14. Is the following sentence true or false? All animals are multicellular.

_____

CHAPTER 7, Living Things *(continued)*

WordWise

Use the clues to identify key terms from Chapter 7. Write the terms on the lines. Then find the words hidden in the puzzle and circle them. Words are across or up-and-down.

Clues	Key Terms
Change that produces a more complex organism	_____
A trace of an ancient organism that has been preserved in rock	_____
The maintenance of stable internal conditions	_____
A dense area in a cell that contains nucleic acids	_____
An organism whose cell lacks a nucleus	_____
A group of organisms that can mate and produce fertile offspring	_____
Change in the surroundings that causes an organism to react	_____
The scientific study of how living things are classified	_____
The one factor in an experiment that the scientist changes	_____

```
e h p r o k a r y o t e j d e y v t a o
h s j i l f b t e h o m e o s t a s i s
d t l s k e t u h g d s m a e t r p u f
o i b p d e v e l o p m e n t f i n r f
a m p e o r d y w o v a r l t o a n y o
r u a c p j i o l g e r x d a v b m u s
p l n i s t w t a x o n o m y p l h r s
a u p e k t u o e d a s p u f c e v r i
h s i s h r a c v n u c l e u s m p r l
```

© Prentice-Hall, Inc.

CHAPTER 8

VIRUSES AND BACTERIA

....

SECTION 8-1 **Viruses** (pages 238-244)

This section describes what viruses are, what they look like, and how they multiply.

▶ What Is a Virus? (pages 238–239)

1. Why do biologists consider viruses to be nonliving? _____

_____

_____

2. Is the following sentence true or false? Viruses multiply the same way as

   other organisms. _____

3. Circle the name of a living thing that provides energy for a virus or an
   organism.

   a. parasite   **b.** host   **c.** bacteriophage   **d.** particle

4. Viruses act like _____ because they destroy the cells in
   which they multiply.

5. What organisms can viruses infect? _____

_____

6. Is the following sentence true or false? Each virus can enter only a few

   types of cells in a few specific species. _____

▶ Naming Viruses (page 239)

7. Why don't scientists use binomial nomenclature to name viruses?

_____

CHAPTER 8, Viruses and Bacteria *(continued)*

8. Circle the letter before each name of a virus.

   a. Ebola   **b.** *Bubo virginianus*

   c. tomato mosaic   **d.** *Clostridium tetani*

▶ The Shapes and Sizes of Viruses (page 240)

9. Is the following sentence true or false? All viruses have the same shape.

   _____

10. A virus that infects bacteria is called a(n) _____.

11. Is the following sentence true or false? Viruses are much smaller than

    bacteria. _____

12. Because viruses are so small, they are measured in units called

    _____.

▶ Structure of Viruses (pages 240–241)

13. Label the two basic parts of a virus in this diagram.

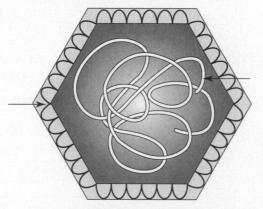

14. What are two functions of a virus's outer protein coat?

    a. _____

    b. _____

15. Is the following sentence true or false? The shape of the proteins allows
    the virus's coat to attach to only certain cells in the host.

    _____

▶ How Viruses Multiply (pages 241–243)

Match the kind of virus with the way it multiplies in a cell. Viruses may be used more than once.

How It Multiplies	Viruses
_____ **16.** The virus's genetic material becomes part of the cell's genetic material.	**a.** active virus
	b. hidden virus
_____ **17.** The virus immediately begins to multiply after entering cell.	
_____ **18.** The virus stays inactive for a long time.	

19. Is the following sentence true or false? When the virus is active, the cell makes the virus's proteins and genetic material and new viruses are

made. _____

▶ Viruses and the Living World (page 244)

20. What are two illnesses caused by viruses? _____

_____

21. Is the following sentence true or false? Viruses can cause diseases only

in humans. _____

22. How are viruses used for gene therapy? _____

_____

_____

Reading Skill Practice

Illustrations in textbooks help illustrate ideas that might be difficult to visualize. Look carefully at the illustration in Figure 4 on page 241. What is this drawing describing? Do your work on a separate sheet of paper.

CHAPTER 8, Viruses and Bacteria *(continued)*

SECTION 8-2 **Bacteria** (pages 246-255)

This section explains what bacteria are, their positive roles, and how they reproduce.

▶ The Bacterial Cell (pages 246–248)

1. Bacteria are _____.The genetic material in their cells is not contained in a nucleus.

2. Is the following sentence true or false? Bacteria are living organisms because they use energy, grow, and respond to their surroundings.

_____

3. What three shapes can bacterial cells have?

a. _____ b. _____ c. _____

4. Circle the letter of the cell structures where proteins are made.

a. cell wall   b. cytoplasm   c. ribosomes   d. flagellum

5. Label the parts of a bacterial cell in this diagram.

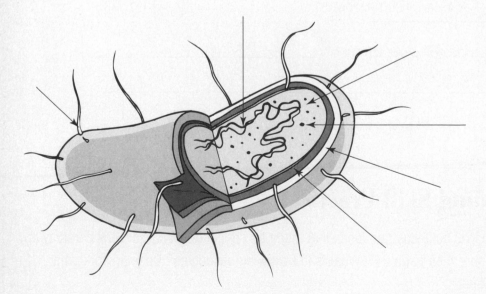

6. Is the following sentence true or false? Bacteria that do not have flagella are never moved from one place to another. _____

▶ Two Kingdoms of Bacteria (pages 248–249)

7. List the two kingdoms into which scientists divide bacteria.

a. _____   b. _____

8. In what kinds of environments are archaebacteria found? _____

_____

_____

_____

9. Circle the letter of each sentence that is true about eubacteria.

a. Eubacteria live in extreme environments.

b. Eubacteria living on your skin cause disease.

c. Eubacteria help maintain some of Earth's physical conditions.

d. Eubacteria help other organisms to survive.

▶ Reproduction in Bacteria (pages 249–250)

10. Complete the table below about reproduction in bacteria.

Reproduction in Bacteria		
	Asexual Reproduction	**Sexual Reproduction**
Name of Process		
Number of Parents		
What Occurs in Process		
Result of Process		

CHAPTER 8, Viruses and Bacteria *(continued)*

▶ Survival Needs (pages 250–251)

11. List the two ways in which autotrophic bacteria make food.

a. _____

b. _____

12. How do heterotrophic bacteria get food? _____

_____

13. Is the following sentence true or false? All bacteria must use oxygen to

break down food for energy. _____

14. When do bacteria form endospores? _____

_____

▶ Bacteria and The Living World (pages 251–255)

15. Circle the letter of each sentence that is true about bacteria.

a. All bacteria are harmful and cause disease.

b. Methane gas produced by archaebacteria living millions of years ago
helps to heat homes.

c. Bacteria help produce foods such as cheese, apple cider, and olives.

d. Bacteria do not cause food to spoil.

16. Soil bacteria that break down large chemicals in dead organisms into

small chemicals are called _____.

17. Is the following sentence true or false? Bacteria are used to clean up oil

spills and gasoline leaks. _____

18. List three ways that bacteria in your digestive system are helpful to you.

a. _____

b. _____

c. _____

19. How do bacteria help people with diabetes? _____

_____

_____

_____

· ·

SECTION 8-3 Viruses, Bacteria, and Your Health
(pages 258-263)

This section explains how diseases are passed from person to person and how these diseases can be treated or prevented.

▶ How Infectious Diseases Spread (pages 258–260)

1. What is an infectious disease? _____

_____

_____

2. Complete this concept map to show how infectious diseases can spread.

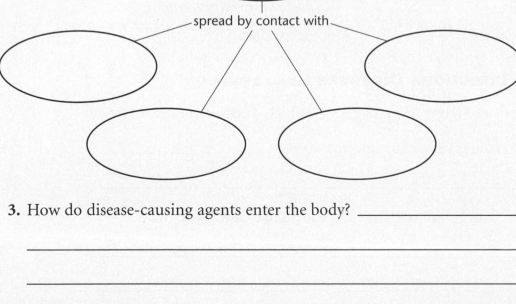

3. How do disease-causing agents enter the body? _____

_____

_____

_____

CHAPTER 8, Viruses and Bacteria *(continued)*

4. Is the following sentence true or false? The flu is spread only by direct

contact, such as kissing a person with the flu. _____

5. Give one example of how objects can spread diseases. _____

_____

_____

_____

Match the animal with the disease that it spreads.

	Disease	Animal
_____	**6.** rabies	**a.** ticks
_____	**7.** Lyme disease	**b.** raccoons
_____	**8.** encephalitis	**c.** mosquitoes

9. Is the following sentence true or false? Some viruses and bacteria that

live in food, water, and soil can cause disease. _____

10. Circle the letter of the bacteria that produces a toxin that can cause
botulism.

a. salmonella

b. *Clostridium botulinum*

c. *Clostridium tetani*

d. encephalitis

▶ Common Infectious Diseases (pages 260–261)

11. Look carefully at Figure 17 on page 261. Which diseases are spread by

contact with contaminated or infected objects? _____

_____

12. From the diseases listed in Figure 17, which are caused by a virus?

_____

_____

_____

13. From Figure 17, describe the symptoms of food poisoning. _____

_____

_____

▶ Treating Infectious Diseases (pages 262–263)

14. Is the following sentence true or false? Diseases caused by viruses can

be cured with antibiotics. _____

15. What is an antibiotic? _____

_____

16. Why are antibiotics less effective now than they once were? _____

_____

_____

▶ Preventing Infectious Diseases (page 263)

17. Is the following sentence true or false? A vaccine activates the body's
natural defenses so that the body is ready to destroy an invading virus

or bacterium. _____

18. What are three diseases that vaccines can protect you from? _____

_____

▶ Staying Healthy (page 263)

19. Circle the letter of each sentence that is true about protecting yourself
from infectious diseases.

   a. Eat nutritious food.

   b. Get plenty of rest, fluids, and exercise.

   c. Share eating utensils or cups.

   d. Get vaccinated.

20. What should you do if you get ill? _____

_____

CHAPTER 8, Viruses and Bacteria *(continued)*

WordWise

Use the clues below to identify key terms from Chapter 8. Write the terms on the lines, putting one letter in each blank. When you finish, the word enclosed in the diagonal lines will reveal the way in which bacteria multiply by asexual reproduction.

Clues

1. A virus that infects bacteria
2. Nonliving particle that invades cells
3. Two bacteria exchange genetic material
4. Harmful organism that lives on a host
5. Breaking down food to release energy
6. Region inside the cell membrane
7. Long, whiplike structure on bacteria

8. Chemical that kills only bacteria
9. Small, rounded, thick-walled, resting cell
10. Energy source for a parasite
11. Poison produced by bacteria
12. Cell part in which proteins are made
13. Stimulates the body to produce chemicals that destroy viruses and bacteria

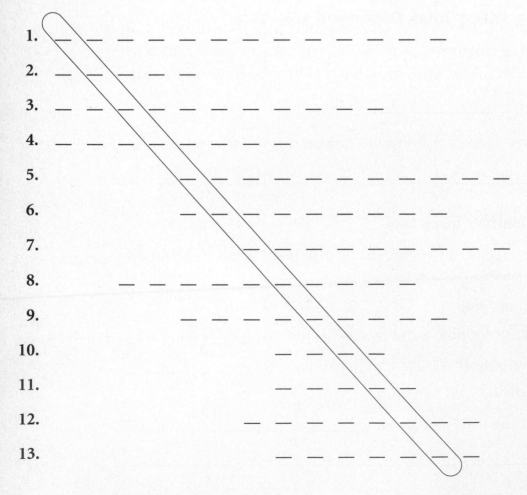

CHAPTER 9

PROTISTS AND FUNGI

SECTION 9-1 **Protists**
(pages 270-279)

This section describes the characteristics of protists.

▶ What Is a Protist? (pages 270–271)

1. Circle the letter of each sentence that is true about protists.

   a. All protists are eukaryotes, organisms that have cells with nuclei.

   b. All protists live in dry surroundings.

   c. All protists are unicellular.

   d. Some protists are heterotrophs, some are autotrophs, and some are both.

2. List the three categories into which scientists group protists.

   a. _____

   b. _____

   c. _____

▶ Animal-like Protists (pages 271–275)

3. Circle the letter of each characteristic that animal-like protists share with animals.

   a. autotroph   **b.** heterotroph   **c.** movement   **d.** unicellular

4. Another name for an animal-like protist is _____.

5. Describe how a sarcodine, such as an ameba, gets food. _____

   _____

   _____

   _____

CHAPTER 9, Protists and Fungi (continued)

6. Circle the letter of the cell part in an ameba that removes excess water.

    a. pseudopod

    b. cilia

    c. contractile vacuole

    d. cell membrane

7. Is the following sentence true or false? Paramecia have two nuclei.

    _____

Match the animal-like protist with the cell part it uses for movement.

	Protist	**Cell Part**
_____	**8.** ameba	**a.** cilia
_____	**9.** paramecium	**b.** flagella
_____	**10.** zooflagellate	**c.** pseudopods

11. Is the following sentence true or false? Zooflagellates living in symbiosis always harm the animal in which they live. _____

12. Animal-like protists called _____ are parasites that feed on the cells and body fluids of their hosts.

13. Is the following sentence true or false? Sporozoans never have more than one host. _____

▶ Funguslike Protists (pages 275–276)

14. Circle the letter of each sentence that is true about funguslike protists.

    a. Like fungi, funguslike protists are heterotrophs.

    b. Funguslike protists do not have cell walls.

    c. Funguslike protists use spores to reproduce.

    d. Funguslike protists never move during their lives.

15. List the three types of funguslike protists.

    a. _____

    b. _____

    c. _____

16. Where do most water molds and downy mildews live? _____

_____

17. Circle the letter of each place where slime molds live.

    a. dry soil   **b.** moist soil   **c.** decaying plants   **d.** in animals

▶ Plantlike Protists (pages 276–279)

18. Plantlike protists are commonly called _____.

19. Like plants, plantlike protists are _____; they make their own food.

20. Complete this table about the different types of plantlike protists.

Characteristics of Plantlike Protists		
Type	**Unicellular or Multicellular**	**Characteristics**
Euglenoids		
Dinoflagellates		
Diatoms		
Green Algae		
Red Algae		
Brown Algae		

📖 Reading Skill Practice

Concept maps are useful in organizing information. Make a concept map to show the characteristics of the four different types of animal-like protists. For more information about concept maps, see page 766 in the Skills Handbook of your textbook. Do your work on a separate sheet of paper.

CHAPTER 9, Protists and Fungi *(continued)*

SECTION 9–2 **Algal Blooms** (pages 280–282)

This section describes how the rapid growth of algae affects ocean water and fresh water.

▶ **Introduction** (page 280)

1. Is the following sentence true or false? A rapid increase in the population

    of algae never harms other organisms. _____

▶ **Saltwater Blooms** (page 281)

2. Circle the letter of each sentence that is true about saltwater algal blooms.

    a. Saltwater algal blooms are commonly called red tides.

    b. The water is red during a red tide because of toxins produced by the algae.

    c. Red tides are never any other color but red.

    d. Dinoflagellates and diatoms are two kinds of algae that often cause red tides.

3. List two conditions that often cause red tides to occur.

    a. _____

    b. _____

4. Why are red tides dangerous to people and other organisms? _____

    _____

    _____

    _____

▶ **Freshwater Blooms** (page 282)

5. In a process called _____, nutrients, such as nitrogen and phosphorus, build up in a lake or pond over time, causing an increase in the growth of algae.

6. Complete the following flowchart to show what occurs when algae grow rapidly in a pond or lake.

Eutrophication

Algae on the water's surface prevent _____ from reaching plants and other algae underwater. These plants _____ and sink to the bottom.

↓

_____ that break down the remains of the dead plants increase in number and use up all the _____ in the water.

↓

Fish and other organisms _____ without the _____ they need to survive.

· ·

Fungi (pages 285-294)

This section explains what fungi are, how they get food, and their role in the environment.

▶ What Are Fungi? (pages 285–286)

1. Circle the letter before each sentence that is true about fungi.

   a. All fungi are multicellular organisms.

   b. Most fungi are eukaryotes.

   c. Most fungi use spores to reproduce.

   d. Most fungi are autotrophs.

2. What are three examples of fungi? _____

_____

_____

CHAPTER 9, Protists and Fungi *(continued)*

▶ Cell Structure (page 286)

3. The cells of fungi are arranged in branching, threadlike tubes called

_____.

4. Is the following sentence true or false? Fuzzy-looking molds that grow

on food have hyphae that are packed tightly together. _____

5. Identify the structures
of the mushroom
shown here.

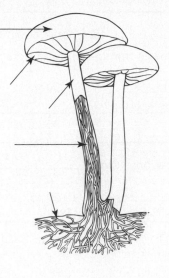

▶ How Do Fungi Obtain Food? (page 287)

6. Describe the process by which a fungus feeds. _____

_____

_____

_____

_____

7. Is the following sentence true or false? Some fungi are parasites.

_____

▶ Reproduction in Fungi (pages 287–288)

8. Fungi most often reproduce by _____.

9. Yeast cells reproduce asexually in a process called _____.

10. Is the following sentence true or false? Fungi reproduce sexually only when conditions become unfavorable. _____

▶ Classification of Fungi (page 289)

11. What two characteristics are used to classify fungi into groups?

a. _____

b. _____

12. What are the four groups of fungi?

a. _____   b. _____

c. _____   d. _____

▶ Fungi and the Living World (pages 292–294)

13. Fungi that are _____ break down the chemicals in dead organisms.

14. Is the following sentence true or false? Certain kinds of fungi cause diseases in plants and in humans. _____

15. Some molds produce _____, substances that kill bacteria.

16. How do some fungi help plants grow larger and healthier? _____

_____

_____

17. An organism that consists of a fungus and either algae or autotrophic bacteria that live together in a mutualistic relationship is a(n)

_____. The fungus provides the algae or autotrophic

bacteria with _____. The algae or autotrophic

bacteria provide the fungus with _____.

18. Look at Figure 19 B on page 294. What are the lichens doing to the rocks?

_____

_____

CHAPTER 9, Protists and Fungi *(continued)*

WordWise

Match each definition on the left with the correct term on the right. Then write the number of each term in the appropriate box below. When you have filled in all the boxes, add up the numbers in each column, row, and two diagonals. The sums should be the same. Some terms may not be used.

A. Asexual reproduction in yeast

B. Temporary bulges of the cell membrane that fill with cytoplasm to move an ameba

C. An interaction between two species where at least one of the species benefits

D. Nutrients build up in a lake over time, causing an increase in algal growth

E. Reproductive hyphae that grow out of a fungus

F. Chemical that produces color

G. An interaction between two species where both partners benefit

H. Hairlike projections from cells that move with a wavelike pattern

I. The rapid growth of a population of algae

1. pseudopod
2. mutualism
3. pigment
4. algal bloom
5. fruiting body
6. budding
7. eutrophication
8. symbiosis
9. cilia
10. spore
11. contractile vacuole
12. lichen

A ___	B ___	C ___
D ___	E ___	F ___
G ___	H ___	I ___

= ___

= ___

= ___

= ___

= ___   = ___   = ___   = ___

___   ___   ___

CHAPTER 10

INTRODUCTION TO PLANTS

SECTION 10–1 **The Plant Kingdom** (pages 300–307)

This section explains the features that all plants have. It also describes what plants need to survive and how they reproduce.

▶ What Is a Plant? (pages 301–302)

1. Circle the letter of each characteristic that all plants share.

    a. heterotroph   **b.** autotroph   **c.** prokaryote   **d.** eukaryote

2. Is the following sentence true or false? Plants make their own food in the

    process of photosynthesis. _____

3. Plant cells have a(n) _____, a boundary that surrounds the cell membrane and separates the cell from the environment.

4. Cell walls are made mostly of _____, a chemical that makes the walls rigid.

5. Label the diagram of the plant cell below.

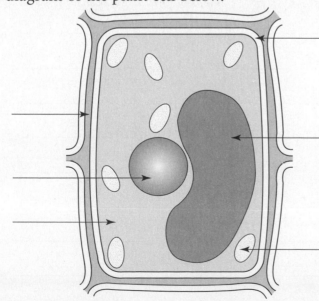

CHAPTER 10, Introduction to Plants *(continued)*

6. Is the following sentence true or false? Only some plants are

   multicellular. _____

7. A group of similar cells that perform a specific function in an organism

   is a(n) _____.

▶ Origin of Plants (page 302)

8. How do biologists learn which organisms were the ancestors of today's

   plants? _____

9. A green pigment found in the chloroplasts of plants is called

   _____.

10. Why do biologists think that ancient green algae were the ancestors of

    today's plants? _____

    _____

▶ Living on Land (pages 303–306)

11. List five things that plants must do to survive on land.

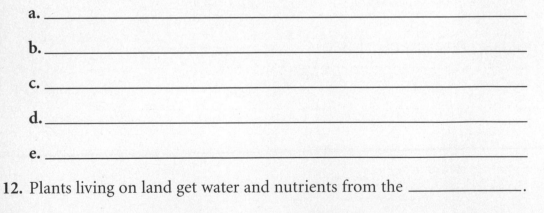

    a. _____

    b. _____

    c. _____

    d. _____

    e. _____

12. Plants living on land get water and nutrients from the _____.

13. Why can a plant on land lose water and dry out? _____

    _____

    _____

    _____

14. Circle the letter of one adaptation that land plants have to keep from drying out.

   a. chlorophyll   **b.** cell wall

   c. cuticle   **d.** vascular tissue

15. Some plants move water, minerals, and food with an internal system of tubelike structures called _____.

16. Is the following sentence true or false? Some land plants are supported by vascular tissue. _____

17. What occurs during fertilization? _____

_____

18. Circle the letter of the name of a fertilized egg.

   a. sporophyte   **b.** gamete

   c. gametophyte   **d.** zygote

▶ **Complex Life Cycles** (page 307)

19. Plants produce spores during the _____ stage and produce gametes during the _____ stage.

20. Is the following sentence true or false? The sporophyte of a plant looks the same as the gametophyte. _____

21. What are two kinds of gametes that a gametophyte produces?

   a. _____   **b.** _____

📖 Reading Skill Practice

A concept map is a useful tool for organizing information. Make a concept map that shows the characteristics shared by all plants described in *What Is a Plant?* on pages 301–302. For more information about concept maps, see page 766 in the Skills Handbook of your textbook. Do your work on a separate sheet of paper.

CHAPTER 10, Introduction to Plants *(continued)*

· ·

SECTION 10–2 **Photosynthesis and Light** (pages 310-314)

This section explains how plants get energy from sunlight and describes what occurs during photosynthesis.

▶ The Nature of Light (pages 310–311)

1. Circle the letter of each sentence that is true about light.

   a. The sun is the source of energy on Earth.

   b. The light you can see is called a prism.

   c. White light is made up of red, orange, yellow, green, blue, and violet light.

   d. Shiny surfaces absorb light and dark surfaces reflect light.

2. A shirt looks red because it _____ red light.

3. The colors of light that make up white light are referred to as the

   _____ .

▶ Plants and Light (pages 311–312)

4. Circle the color of light that is reflected by plant leaves.

   a. green   **b.** red   **c.** yellow   **d.** blue

5. Light is absorbed by _____ found in the chloroplasts of plant cells.

6. Circle the letter of each color of light that is absorbed by chlorophyll.

   a. green   **b.** blue   **c.** yellow   **d.** red

7. Circle the letter of each sentence that is true about plant pigments.

   a. Accessory pigments absorb the same colors of light that chlorophyll does.

   b. Accessory pigments are always visible in plants.

   c. Chlorophyll masks the color of most accessory pigments during most of the year.

   d. In cool temperatures, chlorophyll breaks down and the colors of accessory pigments can be seen.

8. How is the light energy absorbed by plants important to photosynthesis?

_____

_____

▶ **The Chemistry of Photosynthesis** (pages 313–314)

9. In addition to light, what do plants need for photosynthesis?

_____

10. In the diagram below, draw arrows to show which materials the plant is taking up and which materials the plant is giving off or using.

Oxygen

Sunlight

Sugar

Carbon dioxide

Water

11. Write the chemical equation for the process of photosynthesis.

_____

12. What happens to excess food made by plants? _____

_____

📖 Reading Skill Practice

A summary helps you to review the main ideas of something you have read. Write a summary of the subsections *Plants and Light* and *The Chemistry of Photosynthesis*. The summary should be much shorter in length than the actual text. However, the summary should include all the main ideas. Do your work on a separate sheet of paper.

CHAPTER 10, Introduction to Plants *(continued)*

SECTION 10-3 Mosses, Liverworts, and Hornworts *(pages 315-318)*

This section describes the characteristics of plants that do not have vascular tissue.

▶ **Characteristics of Nonvascular Plants** (pages 315–316)

1. List two characteristics of nonvascular plants.

   a. _____

   b. _____

2. Is the following sentence true or false? Nonvascular plants can pass

   materials only from one cell to the next. _____

3. Circle the letter of the structure that provides support for nonvascular plants.

   a. roots   **b.** stems   **c.** vascular tissue   **d.** cell wall

4. Is the following sentence true or false? Nonvascular plants can become

   very large and tall because of their support system. _____

5. How do nonvascular plants get water? _____

   _____

6. Is the following true or false? Nonvascular plants must have water to let

   the sperm cells swim to the egg cells. _____

▶ **Mosses** (pages 316–317)

7. Circle and label the gametophyte and the sporophyte in the diagram of the moss.

8. Thin rootlike structures that anchor moss and absorb water and nutrients from the

   soil are called _____.

9. Describe the sporophyte generation of a moss. _____

_____

_____

_____

10. Circle the letter of each way people use peat moss.

    a. as food   **b.** in gardening   **c.** as a fuel   **d.** as cloth

11. Is the following sentence true or false? Peat moss forms in bogs where dead plants do not decay, but are pressed into layers as they fall to the

    bottom of the bog. _____

12. Why are mosses called pioneer plants? _____

_____

_____

▶ Liverworts and Hornworts (page 318)

13. How do liverworts differ from mosses? _____

_____

14. Is the following sentence true or false? There are more species of

    hornworts than there are liverworts. _____

SECTION 10–4 Ferns and Their Relatives (pages 320–324)

This section describes the characteristics of plants that have vascular tissue, but do not produce seeds.

▶ Characteristics of Seedless Vascular Plants (pages 321–322)

1. List two characteristics that ferns, club mosses, and horsetails share.

    a. _____

    b. _____

CHAPTER 10, Introduction to Plants *(continued)*

2. Circle the letter before each sentence that is true about vascular tissue.

    a. Plants can grow tall without vascular tissue.

    b. Nonvascular plants are better suited to life on land.

    c. Vascular tissue transports water and food throughout a plant's body.

    d. Vascular tissue gives a plant strength and stability.

3. Why must ferns, club mosses, and horsetails grow in moist surroundings?

    _____

    _____

    _____

▶ Ferns (pages 322–323)

4. Is the following sentence true or false? Ferns are small plants that can

    only grow low to the ground. _____

5. The stems of most ferns are located _____. Leaves grow

    _____ from the top side of the stems, and roots grow

    _____ from the bottom of the stems.

6. Label the parts of a fern in this diagram.

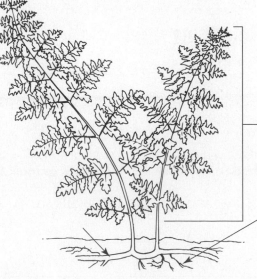

7. Circle the letter of each sentence that is true about the function of roots.

    a. Roots anchor the fern to the ground.

    b. Roots keep the fern from losing water.

    c. Roots produce spores.

    d. Roots absorb water and nutrients from the soil.

8. Fern leaves are called _____.

9. What is the function of the cuticle on the upper surface of fern leaves?

_____

10. Circle the letter of each sentence that is true about reproduction in ferns.

    a. The familiar fern plant with its large fronds is the gametophyte stage.

    b. Spores develop in spore cases on the underside of mature fronds.

    c. Wind and water carry released spores great distances.

    d. Spores will grow into gametophytes in dry, sunny soil.

11. List three ways in which ferns are useful to people.

    a. _____

    b. _____

    c. _____

▶ Club Mosses and Horsetails (page 324)

12. How are club mosses and horsetails similar to ferns? _____

_____

_____

13. Circle the letter before each sentence that is true about club mosses and horsetails.

    a. There are thousands of different species of club mosses and horsetails.

    b. Club mosses today are much smaller than their ancestors were.

    c. Club mosses have jointed stems with long, needlelike branches that grow in a circle around each joint.

    d. Horsetail stems contain silica, a gritty substance also found in sand.

CHAPTER 10, Introduction to Plants (continued)

WordWise

Use the clues to fill in the blanks with key terms from Chapter 10. Then put the numbered letters in the correct spaces to find the hidden message.

Clues

Stage in which plant produces spores

Key Terms

— — — — — — — — —
1   2 3   4

Fern leaf

— — — —
5   6 7

Group of cells that has a specific job

— — — — — —
8 9 10   11

Rootlike structure that anchors moss

— — — — — —
12   13   14

Surrounds cell membrane in plant cells

— — — — — — —
15   16   17   18

Saclike storage area in a plant cell

— — — — — —
19 20   21   22

A sperm or egg cell

— — — — —
23   24 25

Layer of dead mosses compressed at the bottom of a bog

— — — —
26 27 28

Mosses and liverworts are _____ plants.

— — — — — — — — — —
29   30   31   32   33 34

Chemical that makes cell walls rigid

— — — — — — — —
35 36   37 38 39

Hidden Message

— — — — — — — —   — — — — — —   — — —
19 23 10 32 11 22 33 12   3 16 31 6 25 39   27 34 4

— — — —   — — — — — —   — —   — — — —
17 24 36 18   1 21 13 8 26 7   28 38   37 9 5 15

— —   — — — — — .
2 30   35 20 29 14

CHAPTER 11

SEED PLANTS

· ·

SECTION 11–1 The Characteristics of Seed Plants
(pages 330–339)

This section tells about the characteristics of seed plants. It also describes the parts of a seed and the functions of leaves, stems, and roots.

▶ What Is a Seed Plant? (pages 330–331)

1. Circle the letter of each sentence that is true about seed plants.

   a. Seedless plants outnumber seed plants.

   b. Seed plants do not have vascular tissue.

   c. Seed plants use seeds to reproduce.

   d. All seed plants have roots, leaves, and stems.

2. In seed plants, the plants that you see are in the _____

   stage of the life cycle. The _____ stage is microscopic.

▶ Vascular Tissue (page 331)

3. In what two ways does vascular tissue help seed plants to live on land?

   a. _____

   b. _____

4. Circle the letter of the vascular tissue through which food moves.

   a. xylem   **b.** phloem   **c.** roots   **d.** stems

5. Circle the letter of the vascular tissue through which water moves.

   a. xylem   **b.** phloem   **c.** roots   **d.** stems

6. Food made in the plant's _____ travels to the roots and
   stems.

CHAPTER 11, Seed Plants *(continued)*

7. Water and nutrients absorbed by the plant's _____ travel to the stems and leaves.

▶ Seeds (page 332)

8. What is a seed? _____

_____

9. Is the following sentence true or false? Seed plants must have water for

fertilization to occur. _____

Match the part of the seed with its function.

Seed Part	Function
_____ 10. embryo	a. Keeps the seed from drying out
_____ 11. cotyledon	b. Young plant that develops from the fertilized egg
_____ 12. seed coat	c. A seed leaf that stores food

▶ Seed Dispersal (page 333)

13. What do seeds need to develop into a new plant? _____

_____

14. Is the following sentence true or false? Seeds can begin to grow in any

place they land. _____

15. Complete the concept map to show ways that seeds are scattered.

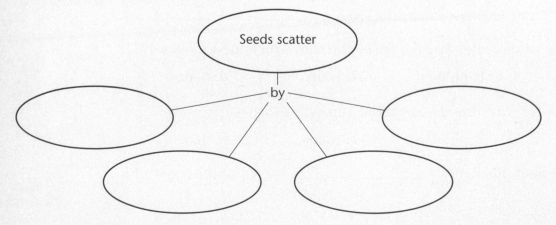

Science Explorer *Focus on Life Science*

▶ Germination (page 334)

16. What is germination? _____

_____

17. Circle the letter before each sentence that is true about germination.

    a. All seeds germinate immediately after they are dispersed.

    b. The embryo uses its stored food to begin to grow.

    c. First, the embryo's leaves and stem grow upward.

    d. Seeds that are dispersed far away from the parent have a better chance of survival.

▶ Leaves (pages 334–336)

18. What role do leaves play in a plant? _____

_____

_____

Look at the structure of a leaf in *Exploring a Leaf* on page 335. Match the leaf part with its function.

Leaf Part	Function
_____ **19.** cuticle	**a.** Spaces between these cells temporarily store carbon dioxide and oxygen
_____ **20.** xylem	**b.** Carries water from the roots to the leaves
_____ **21.** phloem	**c.** Waxy, waterproof coating that covers the leaf's upper surface
_____ **22.** stomata	**d.** Contain chloroplasts
_____ **23.** lower leaf cells	**e.** Carries food made in the leaves to the rest of the plant
_____ **24.** upper leaf cells	**f.** Tiny pores that open and close to let carbon dioxide in and water vapor and oxygen out

25. Is the following sentence true or false? The cells that contain the most

chloroplasts are near the leaf's upper surface. _____

CHAPTER 11, Seed Plants *(continued)*

26. The process by which water evaporates from a plant's leaves is called

    _____.

27. Is the following sentence true or false? On very hot days, the stomata

    often open to keep the plant from losing water. _____

▶ Stems (pages 336–338)

28. List three functions of stems.

    a. _____

    b. _____

    c. _____

29. Is the following sentence true or false? Herbaceous stems are hard and

    rigid and have an outer layer called bark. _____

30. Circle the letter before the cell layer that produces new phloem and xylem.

    a. heartwood   **b.** sapwood   **c.** bark   **d.** cambium

31. What is heartwood? _____

    _____

32. Circle the letter before the tissue that makes up a tree's annual rings.

    a. xylem   **b.** phloem   **c.** cambium   **d.** bark

33. Is the following sentence true or false? One year's growth of a tree is
    represented by one pair of light and dark rings in the tree's stem.

    _____

▶ Roots (pages 338–339)

34. List three functions of roots.

    a. _____

    b. _____

    c. _____

35. Look at the two types of root systems illustrated below. Label the roots as taproot or fibrous roots.

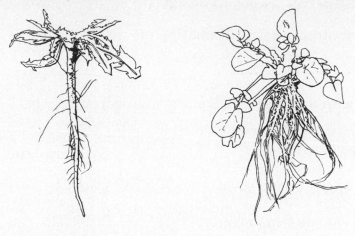

_____   _____

Match the root structure with its function.

Root Structure	Function
_____ **36.** root cap	**a.** Moves food to the roots
_____ **37.** root hairs	**b.** Protects the root from injury during growth
_____ **38.** phloem	**c.** Moves water and nutrients to the stems and leaves
_____ **39.** xylem	**d.** Increase the surface area of the root

SECTION 11–2 **Gymnosperms** (pages 340–345)

This section gives examples of the group of seed plants known as gymnosperms and describes their features and how they reproduce.

▶ **What Are Gymnosperms?** (page 340)

1. What is a gymnosperm? _____

_____

2. Is the following sentence true or false? Gymnosperms have seeds that

do not have a protective covering. _____

CHAPTER 11, Seed Plants *(continued)*

▶ Types of Gymnosperms (pages 341–342)

3. Is the following sentence true or false? Gymnosperms are the oldest

   type of seed plant. _____

Match the gymnosperms with their features. Some gymnosperms may be
used more than once.

Features	Gymnosperms
_____ 4. Only one species exists today.	**a.** cycads
_____ 5. These are cone-bearing plants.	**b.** ginkgo
_____ 6. These plants live only in hot, dry deserts.	**c.** gnetophytes
_____ 7. These plants are found only in tropical areas.	**d.** conifers
_____ 8. Most keep their needles year round.	
_____ 9. These plants look like palm trees with cones.	
_____ 10. Often planted along city streets because they tolerate air pollution.	

▶ Reproduction (pages 342–344)

11. Most gymnosperms have reproductive structures called _____.

12. Is the following sentence true or false? Male cones contain ovules at the

    base of each scale. _____

13. What is pollen? _____

    _____

14. A structure that contains an egg cell is a(n) _____.

15. What happens during pollination? _____

    _____

16. Is the following sentence true or false? Cones that have immature seeds

    point upward. _____

17. Study *Exploring the Life Cycle of a Gymnosperm* on page 344. Then complete the cycle diagram showing the steps in the reproduction of gymnosperms.

A pine tree produces male and

female _____.

The seeds that land in a suitable place will

grow into new _____.

After fertilization, the _____ develops and the seed forms on the scale.

_____ carries seeds away.

When _____ are mature, the scales open.

▶ Gymnosperms and the Living World (page 345)

18. Circle the letter of each product that conifers provide.

a. fruit   **b.** paper   **c.** turpentine   **d.** cotton fibers

19. Is the following sentence true or false? Clear cutting a forest for lumber

prevents the loss of soil and homes for wildlife. _____

SECTION 11-3 Angiosperms (pages 346-351)

This section describes the type of seed plants that produce fruit and their life cycle. It also explains the difference between two groups of plants that produce different kinds of seeds.

▶ What Are Angiosperms? (pages 346–347)

1. A plant that produces seeds that are enclosed in a fruit is called a(n)

_____.

2. Circle the letter of the reproductive structure of an angiosperm.

a. seed   **b.** flower   **c.** petals   **d.** sepals

CHAPTER 11, Seed Plants *(continued)*

3. List two characteristics of angiosperms.

   a. _____

   b. _____

▶ **The Structure of Flowers** (pages 347–348)

Match the parts of the flower with their function.

Function	Flower Parts
_____ 4. Male reproductive parts	**a.** petals
_____ 5. Protect the developing flower	**b.** sepals
_____ 6. Female reproductive parts	**c.** stamens
_____ 7. Colorful structures that attract insects	**d.** pistils

8. Label the parts of the flower in this diagram.

▶ **Reproduction** (pages 348–349)

9. When a flower is pollinated, a grain of pollen falls on a(n)

   _____.

10. In what part of the flower do the sperm cell and the egg cell join together?

_____

11. Is the following sentence true or false? All angiosperms rely on wind for

pollination. _____

12. Describe how animals help to pollinate flowers. _____

_____

_____

_____

▶ Types of Angiosperms (page 350)

13. What are the two major groups of angiosperms?

a. _____ b. _____

14. The embryo in a seed gets food from the _____, or seed
leaf.

Match each characteristic with the type of angiosperm. Each type of
angiosperm may be used more than once.

Characteristics	Types of Angiosperms
_____ **15.** Have only one seed leaf	**a.** monocots
_____ **16.** Have two seed leaves	**b.** dicots
_____ **17.** Flower petals are in fours or fives.	
_____ **18.** Flower petals are in threes.	
_____ **19.** Leaves are wide with branching veins.	
_____ **20.** Leaves are narrow with parallel veins.	
_____ **21.** Roses, violets, and oak trees are examples.	
_____ **22.** Corn, wheat, and tulips are examples.	

▶ Angiosperms and the Living World (page 351)

23. Circle the letter of each product made from angiosperms.

a. furniture   b. clothing   c. turpentine   d. steel

CHAPTER 11, Seed Plants *(continued)*

24. Is the following sentence true or false? Medicines, such as aspirin and

digitalis, come from angiosperms. _____

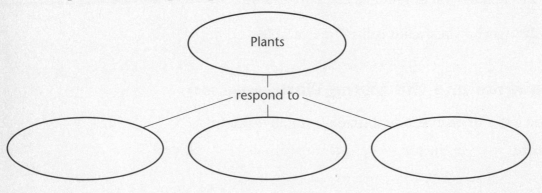

Reading Skill Practice

A compare/contrast table is a useful tool for organizing similarities and differences. Make a table to organize the similarities and differences of monocots and dicots. Use *Characteristics, Monocots,* and *Dicots* as the headings for the columns of the table. For more information about compare/contrast tables, see page 766 in the Skills Handbook of your textbook. Do your work on a separate sheet of paper.

SECTION 11–4 **Plant Responses and Growth** (pages 354-356)

This section explains how plants respond to stimuli in their environment. It also describes the role of plant hormones and the life spans of flowering seed plants.

▶ **Tropisms** (pages 354–355)

1. What is a tropism? _____

_____

2. Is the following sentence true or false? If a plant grows toward the

stimulus, it shows a negative tropism. _____

3. Complete the concept map to show the stimuli to which plants respond.

Plants

respond to

( )   ( )   ( )

▶ **Plant Hormones** (page 355)

4. A chemical that affects how a plant grows and develops is a(n)

_____.

5. What do plant hormones control?

a. _____

b. _____

c. _____

d. _____

e. _____

6. Auxin is a plant hormone that _____ the rate at which a plant's cells grow.

7. Describe how auxin controls a plant's response to light. _____

_____

_____

_____

_____

▶ **Life Spans of Angiosperms** (pages 355–356)

8. Circle the letter of the flowering plants that complete a life cycle within one growing season.

a. perennials   b. biennials   c. annuals   d. centennials

9. Is the following sentence true or false? Most annuals have woody stems.

_____

10. Circle the letter of each sentence that is true about biennials.

a. Biennials complete their life cycle in two years.

b. In the first year, biennials produce seeds and flowers.

c. In the second year, biennials germinate and grow roots.

d. Once the flower produces seeds, the biennial dies.

CHAPTER 11, Seed Plants *(continued)*

11. How long is the life cycle of a perennial? _____

_____

12. Circle the letter of the plant that is a perennial.

    a. parsley   **b.** peony   **c.** cucumber   **d.** petunia

••

SECTION 11–5   Feeding the World (pages 358–360)

This section describes different ways farmers can produce more crops.

▶ Introduction (page 358)

1. List three ways scientists and farmers are working to grow enough food to feed the growing population of people.

    a. _____

_____

    b. _____

_____

    c. _____

_____

▶ Producing Better Plants (page 359)

2. What are the four major sources of food for people? _____

_____

3. Is the following sentence true or false? Farmers can easily feed more

people without increasing the production of crops. _____

4. What two challenges do farmers face in producing more crops?

    a. _____

    b. _____

5. Scientists change an organism's genetic material to produce an

organism with useful qualities in the process of _____.

▶ Improving the Efficiency of Farms (pages 359–360)

6. Is the following sentence true or false? In precision farming, farmers know

how much water and fertilizer different fields need. _____

7. Complete the flowchart to show the process of precision farming.

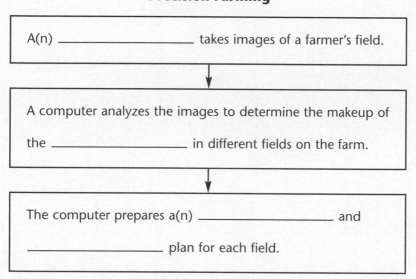

Precision Farming

A(n) _____ takes images of a farmer's field.

A computer analyzes the images to determine the makeup of

the _____ in different fields on the farm.

The computer prepares a(n) _____ and

_____ plan for each field.

8. List three ways in which precision farming benefits farmers.

a. _____ b. _____ c. _____

9. Is the following sentence true or false? Precision farming benefits the

environment by using more fertilizer than the soil needs. _____

▶ Hydroponics (page 360)

10. What is hydroponics? _____

_____

_____

11. Is the following sentence true or false? Hydroponics can be used to

grow crops in places with poor soil. _____

CHAPTER 11, Seed Plants (continued)

WordWise

How fast can you solve this crossword puzzle? You'll need to use what you've learned about seed plants. Go!

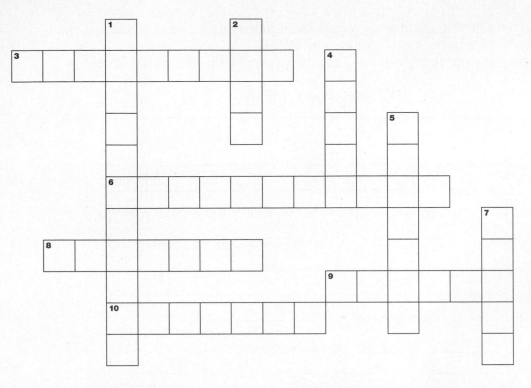

Clues down

1. A method by which plants are grown in solutions of nutrients instead of soil
2. The reproductive structure in gymnosperms
4. A ripened ovary that encloses one or more seeds
5. A plant's growth response
7. Vascular tissue through which water and nutrients travel

Clues across

3. Seed leaf in which food is stored
6. The transfer of pollen from a male structure to a female structure
8. Angiosperms with only one seed leaf
9. The female part of a flower
10. Layer of cells just inside the phloem that divide to produce new phloem and xylem

CHAPTER 12

SPONGES, CNIDARIANS, AND WORMS

SECTION 12-1 **What Is an Animal?**
(pages 366-372)

This section explains the four characteristics of animals and how biologists classify animals into groups. It also describes some animal adaptations.

▶ Characteristics of Animals (pages 367–368)

1. A group of organisms that can mate with each other and produce offspring,

   who in turn can mate and reproduce is a(n) _____.

2. What are the four characteristics of animals?

   a. _____

   b. _____

   c. _____

   d. _____

3. Complete the flowchart to show how cells are organized in animals.

Levels of Organization

Animal cells are grouped together to form a(n) _____,
which has a specific job in the body.

↓

Tissues combine to form a(n) _____, which performs a
more complex job than each tissue by itself.

↓

Organs combine to form a(n) _____.

CHAPTER 12, Sponges, Cnidarians, and Worms *(continued)*

4. Circle the letter of the name of an organ.

   a. muscle cell   **b.** nervous tissue

   c. thigh bone   **d.** skeletal system

5. Every animal is a(n) _____; it cannot make food for itself.

Green plants are _____; they can make their own food.

6. Is the following sentence true or false? Most animals have a cavity inside their body where food is broken down into substances the body

can use. _____

7. What is sexual reproduction? _____

_____

_____

_____

8. The joining of the egg and sperm is called _____.

9. Is the following sentence true or false? When sperm and egg unite, the resulting new individual does not have any characteristics from either

parent. _____

10. What is asexual reproduction? _____

_____

_____

11. Is the following sentence true or false? Asexual reproduction involves

the joining of sex cells from two parents. _____

12. What are most animal movements related to?

   a. _____   **b.** _____   **c.** _____

13. Is the following sentence true or false? Some animals don't move from

place to place. _____

▶ How Animals Meet Their Needs (page 369)

Match the needs with how animals use them.

Use in Animals	Needs

_____ 14. Gives animals raw materials for growth and energy

a. water

b. food

_____ 15. Used in the chemical reactions that keep animals alive

c. oxygen

_____ 16. Releases the energy from food

17. Animals get water, food, and oxygen from their _____.

18. Is the following sentence true or false? An animal's body and behaviors

allow it to respond to its environment. _____

19. What is an adaptation? _____

_____

_____

▶ Adaptations for Getting Food (pages 369–370)

Match the type of animal with what it eats.

Type of Animal	What It Eats

_____ 20. herbivore

a. Both plants and animals

_____ 21. carnivore

b. Only animals

c. Only plants

_____ 22. omnivore

23. Is the following sentence true or false? Herbivores have sharp and

pointed teeth for grinding tough plants. _____

24. Carnivores that hunt and kill other animals are called

_____. The animals that these carnivores capture and

feed upon are called _____.

CHAPTER 12, Sponges, Cnidarians, and Worms *(continued)*

▶ Adaptations for Escaping Predators *(page 370)*

25. Circle the letter of each sentence that is true about adaptations for escaping predators.

    a. Hard shells or spiny skins protect some animals from being eaten by predators.

    b. Skunks "play dead" to protect themselves from predators.

    c. Predators usually attack animals that "play dead."

    d. Predators learn to avoid animals with stingers, claws, bitter-tasting flesh, and smelly sprays.

▶ Classification of Animals *(pages 370–372)*

26. Biologists classify animals in the animal kingdom into about 35 major groups, each of which is called a(n) _____.

27. Look at the branching tree of animal phyla in Figure 6 on page 371. Circle the letter of the animal group that is most closely related to fishes.

    a. sponges   **b.** echinoderms

    c. crustaceans   **d.** amphibians

28. Is the following sentence true or false? Scientists think that all animals arose from single-celled ancestors. _____

29. What do biologists look at when they classify an animal?

    a. _____

    b. _____

    c. _____

30. Is the following sentence true or false? An animal that does not have a backbone is called a vertebrate. _____

31. Circle the letter of the animal that is a vertebrate.

    a. bird   **b.** jellyfish   **c.** spider   **d.** crab

Reading Skill Practice

Illustrations and photographs help explain ideas that you read about. Look at Figure 7 on page 372. What is this illustration communicating? Do your work on a separate sheet of paper.

SECTION
12-2
Symmetry
(pages 373-375)

This section explains that animal bodies have a balanced arrangement.

▶ **Introduction** (page 373)

1. The balanced arrangement of a butterfly's body is called

_____.

▶ **The Mathematics of Symmetry** (page 374)

2. Complete the drawing of the butterfly's body on the other side of the line of symmetry.

3. Because the butterfly can be divided into two halves that are mirror

images of each other, it has _____ symmetry.

4. Objects with many lines of symmetry that all go through a central

point have _____ symmetry.

CHAPTER 12, Sponges, Cnidarians, and Worms *(continued)*

5. Circle the letter of each object that has radial symmetry.

   a. oak leaf **b.** sea anemone **c.** pair of eyeglasses **d.** bicycle wheel

▶ Symmetry in Animals (pages 374–375)

6. Is the following sentence true or false? The bodies of complex animals

   all have either radial or bilateral symmetry. _____

7. Is the following sentence true or false? Animals with radial symmetry

   have distinct front and back ends. _____

8. Circle the letter of each sentence that is true about animals with bilateral symmetry.

   a. Human bodies have bilateral symmetry.

   b. Radially symmetrical animals are larger and more complex than those with bilateral symmetry.

   c. Bilateral symmetry allows for a streamlined, balanced body that moves quickly and efficiently.

   d. Most bilaterally symmetrical animals have sense organs in their back ends.

SECTION 12–3 Sponges and Cnidarians (pages 378-383)

This section describes the characteristics of sponges and cnidarians. It also explores life on a coral reef.

▶ Sponges (pages 378–380)

1. Is the following sentence true or false? People once thought that sponges

   were plants. _____

2. Why are sponges classified as animals? _____

   _____

   _____

3. Describe the body of a sponge. _____

_____

4. Circle the letter of each sentence that is true about how sponges get food and oxygen.

   a. Sponges remove bacteria and protists from the water that enters them.

   b. Pores in the sponge's body trap food particles and digest them.

   c. A sponge gets oxygen from water.

   d. Oxygen is more highly concentrated in the sponge's cells than in the water.

5. A network of _____ supports the bodies of most sponges.

6. Sponges reproduce asexually in a process called _____.

7. Is the following sentence true or false? Sponges have separate sexes.

   _____

▶ **Cnidarians** (pages 381–382)

8. What are cnidarians? _____

_____

9. Circle the letter of each sentence that is true about cnidarians.

   a. Cnidarians are carnivores.

   b. Cnidarians have stinging cells to capture prey.

   c. Cnidarians do not have specialized tissues.

   d. Cnidarians cannot move.

10. Circle the letter of each example of a polyp.

   a. hydra   **b.** sea anemone   **c.** jellyfish   **d.** coral

11. Is the following sentence true or false? A medusa is adapted for a life

   attached to an underwater surface. _____

12. How does a cnidarian capture prey? _____

_____

_____

CHAPTER 12, Sponges, Cnidarians, and Worms *(continued)*

13. In this diagram, identify which body form is a polyp and which is a medusa. Then label the mouth and central cavity for each.

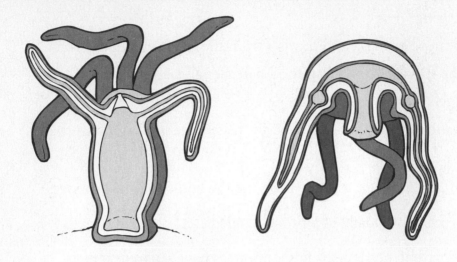

_____   _____

▶ Life on a Coral Reef *(page 383)*

14. Coral reefs are built by _____.

15. Circle the letter of each sentence that is true about coral reefs.

   a. Coral polyps produce hard, stony skeletons around their soft bodies.

   b. When coral polyps die, their skeletons break down to dust.

   c. Coral reefs are very limited in size.

   d. Coral reefs are home to more species of fishes and invertebrates than any other environment on Earth.

· ·

SECTION 12–4

Worms *(pages 385–391)*

This section tells about the characteristics of the three main groups of worms.

▶ What Worms Have in Common *(pages 385–386)*

1. The ability to regrow body parts is called _____.

2. Complete the concept map to show the three major groups of worms.

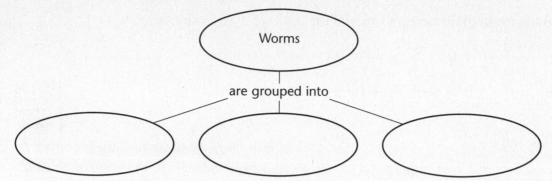

3. List five characteristics shared by all worms.

a. _____

b. _____

c. _____

d. _____

e. _____

4. Circle the letter of each sentence that is true about worms.

a. Worms do not have brains.

b. A worm has sense organs in its head end to respond to food, mates, and predators.

c. Worms can only reproduce sexually.

d. In some worm species, each individual has both male and female sex organs.

▶ **Flatworms** (pages 386–388)

5. Circle the letter of each characteristic of most flatworms.

    a. flat bodies   **b.** round bodies   **c.** parasites   **d.** hosts

6. An organism that lives inside or on another organism and takes its food

from that organism is a(n) _____.

7. Is the following sentence true or false? A parasite has no affect on its

host. _____

CHAPTER 12, Sponges, Cnidarians, and Worms *(continued)*

8. Complete the cycle diagram to show the life cycle of a dog tapeworm.

A dog eats the meat of a rabbit that is infected

with _____.

A rabbit eats grass with the

_____ and becomes

infected with _____.

In the dog's digestive tract, the immature tapeworm attaches to the lining of the dog's

_____.

Fertilized eggs leave the dog's body

along with _____.

The attached tapeworm grows and

produces _____ and

_____.

9. Where do free-living flatworms live? _____

_____

10. Circle the letter of each characteristic of planarians.

    a. parasite   **b.** scavenger   **c.** herbivore   **d.** carnivore

11. Is the following sentence true or false? Planarians rely on their eyesight

    to find food. _____

12. Describe how a planarian feeds. _____

_____

_____

▶ Roundworms *(pages 388–389)*

13. Circle the letter of each sentence that is true about roundworms.

    a. Roundworms can live in nearly any dry environment.

    b. Roundworms have flat bodies.

    c. Roundworms can be carnivores, herbivores, or parasites.

    d. Roundworms have a digestive system that is like a tube, open at both ends.

14. Wastes exit a roundworm's digestive system through an opening called

the _____.

15. What is the advantage of an "assembly line" digestive system? _____

_____

_____

_____

▶ **Segmented Worms** (pages 389–391)

16. Circle the letter of each sentence that is true about segmented worms.

   a. Segmented worms are closely related to flatworms.

   b. Most segmented worms live in burrows or tubes.

   c. Segmented worms have bodies made up of many linked sections.

   d. Reproductive organs are found in every segment of an earthworm.

17. Earthworms have a digestive system with _____ opening(s).

18. What is the advantage of a closed circulatory system? _____

_____

_____

19. An earthworm has five paired pumping organs that act like

_____.

20. Circle the letter of each characteristic of earthworms.

   a. scavenger   **b.** predator

   c. get oxygen through skin   **d.** live in water

21. Is the following sentence true or false? An earthworm crawls forward by

sticking its bristles in the ground and pulling itself along. _____

22. How do earthworms improve the soil? _____

_____

_____

CHAPTER 12, Sponges, Cnidarians, and Worms *(continued)*

WordWise

Answer the questions by writing the correct key terms in the blanks. Use the circled letter from each term to find the hidden key term. Then write a definition for the hidden key term.

1. What is a carnivore that hunts and kills other animals?

_ _ _ _ _ _ Ⓞ _

2. What is a bowl-shaped cnidarian that is adapted for a free-swimming life?

Ⓞ _ _ _ _ _

3. What is the ability to regrow body parts?

_ _ _ _ Ⓞ _ _ _ _ _ _ _

4. What is the symmetry shown by objects if there is a line that divides the object into halves that are mirror images?

_ Ⓞ _ _ _ _ _ _   _ _ _ _ _ _ _ _

5. What is an immature form of an animal that looks very different from the adult?

_ _ _ Ⓞ _

6. What is an organism that must get food by eating other organisms?

_ _ _ _ _ Ⓞ _ _ _ _ _

7. What is an animal that has a backbone?

_ _ Ⓞ _ _ _ _ _ _ _

8. What is an organism that lives inside or on another organism?

_ _ _ _ _ _ _ Ⓞ

Key Term: _ _ _ _ _ _ _ _

Definition: _____

_____

CHAPTER 13

MOLLUSKS, ARTHROPODS, AND ECHINODERMS

....

SECTION 13-1 Mollusks
(pages 398-402)

This section describes the features of mollusks and identifies three major groups of mollusks.

▶ **What Are Mollusks?** (pages 398–399)

1. Circle the letter of each characteristic of a mollusk.

   a. vertebrate   **b.** invertebrate

   c. segmented body   **d.** unsegmented body

2. Give the function of each of the following parts of a mollusk.

   hard outer shell: _____

   mantle: _____

   foot: _____

3. Is the following sentence true or false? Mollusks are found only in dry

   places on land. _____

4. Mollusks have _____ symmetry.

Match the body part with its function.

Body Part	Function
_____ 5. kidneys	**a.** Organs that remove oxygen from water
_____ 6. gills	**b.** A flexible ribbon of tiny teeth that scrapes food from a surface
_____ 7. cilia	**c.** Organs that remove the wastes produced by an animal's cells
_____ 8. radula	**d.** Tiny, hairlike structures that move water over the gills

CHAPTER 13, Mollusks, Arthropods, and Echinoderms *(continued)*

▶ Evidence of Early Mollusks (page 399)

9. How do scientists know that mollusks lived in Earth's oceans about 540

million years ago? _____

_____

10. Is the following sentence true or false? Some kinds of limestone are

partially made from ancient mollusks. _____

▶ Snails and Their Relatives (page 400)

11. List the characteristics that biologists use to classify mollusks.

a. _____   b. _____

c. _____   d. _____

e. _____

12. Complete the concept map to show the three major groups of mollusks.

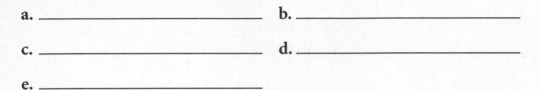
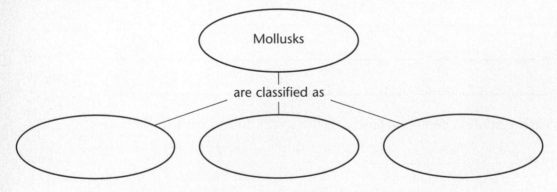

13. Mollusks that have a single shell or no shell at all are called

_____ .

14. How do some snails protect themselves from predators or from dry

conditions? _____

_____

_____

▶ Two-Shelled Mollusks (pages 400–402)

15. What are bivalves? _____

_____

16. How are bivalves different from other mollusks? _____

_____

_____

17. Circle the letter of each sentence that is true about bivalves.

    a. Bivalves use their gills to capture food as they breathe.

    b. Bivalves live on land.

    c. Scallops can move by clapping their shells together and leaping.

    d. A pearl forms in an oyster to protect the oyster from predators.

▶ Mollusks with Tentacles (page 402)

18. Mollusks whose feet are adapted to form tentacles around their mouths

    are _____.

Match the cephalopod with its type of shell.

	Cephalopod	Shell
_____	**19.** nautilus	**a.** Small shell inside the body
_____	**20.** squid	**b.** No shell
_____	**21.** octopus	**c.** Shell outside the body

22. How do cephalopods find and capture food? _____

_____

23. Circle the letter of each sentence that is true about cephalopods.

    a. Cephalopods have large eyes and a complex nervous system.

    b. Cephalopods cannot remember things.

    c. All cephalopods live in the ocean.

    d. Cephalopods swim by waving their tentacles.

CHAPTER 13, Mollusks, Arthropods, and Echinoderms *(continued)*

📖 Reading Skill Practice

A flowchart is useful for organizing the steps in a process. Make a flowchart that shows the steps in the process of forming limestone rock from mollusk shells. You can find this information in *Evidence of Early Mollusks* on page 399. For more information about flowcharts, see page 767 in the Skills Handbook of your textbook. Do your work on a separate sheet of paper.

●●

SECTION 13-2 **Arthropods** (pages 404–411)

This section describes the characteristics of arthropods, and tells about the major groups of arthropods.

▶ Characteristics of Arthropods (pages 405–407)

1. What are the characteristics of an arthropod? _____

_____

_____

2. Circle the letter of each appendage found in arthropods.

   a. wings   **b.** circulatory system   **c.** mouthparts   **d.** legs

3. How does an exoskeleton help arthropods live on land? _____

_____

_____

4. Exoskeletons are made of _____, a polymer that is tough and flexible.

5. What happens to the exoskeleton when an arthropod grows? _____

_____

_____

6. Look at the table in Figure 6. Crustaceans have _____

pairs of antennae. Arachnids have _____ body segments.

Insects have _____ pairs of legs.

7. Is the following sentence true or false? Joints in their appendages give

arthropods flexibility and the ability to move. _____

Match the type of appendage with its function.

Appendage	Function
_____ 8. mouthparts	a. Crushing food
_____ 9. antennae	b. Walking, catching prey, defending against predators
_____ 10. legs	c. Have sense organs for smelling, tasting, and touching

▶ Origin of Arthropods (page 407)

11. What evidence shows biologists that arthropods and segmented worms

are not closely related? _____

_____

12. Is the following sentence true or false? Arthropods first arose in the

oceans. _____

▶ Crustaceans (pages 407–409)

13. List the five major groups of arthropods.

a. _____ b. _____ c. _____

d. _____ e. _____

14. What is a crustacean? _____

_____

_____

15. Crustacean larvae develop into adults by _____,
a process in which an animal's body changes in form during its life cycle.

CHAPTER 13, Mollusks, Arthropods, and Echinoderms *(continued)*

16. Circle the letter of each sentence that is true about crustaceans.

    a. Crustaceans get oxygen through gills.

    b. Crustaceans live only in dry areas on land.

    c. The pistil shrimp eats dead plants and animals.

    d. Krill are herbivores that eat plantlike microorganisms.

▶ Spiders and Their Relatives (pages 408–410)

17. An arthropod with only two body sections is a(n) _____.

18. Circle the letter of each characteristic of arachnids.

    a. Abdomen with reproductive organs and digestive tract

    b. Eight legs

    c. Four antennae

    d. Book lungs

19. Write the name of the arachnid in each drawing.

_____ _____   _____

20. Circle the letter of each sentence that is true about spiders.

    a. All spiders are herbivores.

    b. All spiders build webs.

    c. Spiders have hollow fangs that inject venom into prey.

    d. Spiders rarely bite people.

Science Explorer Focus on Life Science

21. Circle the letter of the name of a mite.

    a. black widow   **b.** chigger   **c.** brown recluse   **d.** tarantula

22. Ticks are _____ that live on the outside of a host animal's body.

23. When are scorpions most active? _____

_____

24. A scorpion has a(n) _____ at the end of its abdomen to inject venom into prey.

▶ **Centipedes and Millipedes** (page 411)

Match the arthropod with its characteristics. Each kind of arthropod may be used more than once.

Characteristics	Arthropods
_____ **25.** Two pairs of legs on each segment	**a.** centipede
_____ **26.** One pair of legs on each segment	**b.** millipede
_____ **27.** Predators with sharp jaws	
_____ **28.** Herbivores	

SECTION 13-3 **Insects** (pages 412–417)

This section describes the characteristics of insects and how insects affect people.

▶ **The Insect Body** (page 413)

1. What is an insect? _____

_____

_____

2. Circle the letter of the body segment to which wings and legs are attached.

    a. head   **b.** thorax   **c.** abdomen   **d.** exoskeleton

CHAPTER 13, Mollusks, Arthropods, and Echinoderms (continued)

3. Identify the body segments of the grasshopper below.

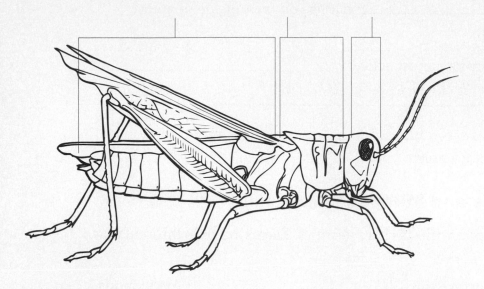

4. Insects have two _____ eyes, which contain many lenses.

5. Insects get oxygen into their bodies through a system of _____.

▶ From Egg to Adult (pages 413–415)

6. Complete the cycle diagram to show the stages of complete metamorphosis.

Insect life begins as a tiny, hard-shelled,

fertilized _____.

When its development is complete, the

_____ leaves the pupal

case. It feeds and finds mates.

Immature form of an animal that looks very different from the adult is a(n)

_____.

The insect is enclosed in a protective covering. The insect at this stage is called a(n)

_____.

7. In gradual metamorphosis, the egg hatches into a(n) _____, which looks much like a small adult.

▶ How Insects Feed (page 414)

8. Is the following sentence true or false? If it is living, or if it once was living, some kind of insect will eat it. _____

9. Insects get food using _____ that are highly specialized.

▶ Defending Themselves (page 416)

10. What are four ways that insects protect themselves from predators?

_____

_____

_____

_____

11. The most common defense insects have is _____, in which the insect blends with its surroundings so that it is nearly invisible.

▶ Insects and Humans (pages 416–417)

12. Is the following sentence true or false? Most insects are harmful to people. _____

13. What are two ways in which insects are helpful? _____

_____

_____

_____

▶ Controlling Insect Pests (page 417)

14. Is the following sentence true or false? Pesticides used to kill harmful insects will also kill helpful insects and can harm other animals.

_____

15. Introducing natural insect predators or natural insect diseases is a method of getting rid of harmful insects called _____.

CHAPTER 13, Mollusks, Arthropods, and Echinoderms *(continued)*

SECTION 13-4 **The Sounds of Insects**
(pages 420-422)

This section explains how insects make sounds and why they make them.

▶ **How Is Sound Produced?** (pages 420–421)

1. How are all sounds made? _____

_____

2. Is the following sentence true or false? Sound waves can travel only

through air. _____

▶ **Communicating by Sound** (page 422)

3. What are two ways in which insects make sounds? _____

_____

_____

4. Why do insects make sounds? _____

_____

SECTION 13-5 **Echinoderms**
(pages 423-426)

This section tells about spiny-skinned animals called echinoderms.

▶ **The "Spiny Skinned" Animals** (pages 423–424)

1. What is an echinoderm? _____

_____

2. The skin of most echinoderms is supported by a spiny internal skeleton,

called a(n) _____.

Science Explorer *Focus on Life Science*

3. What is a water vascular system? _____

_____

▶ Sea Stars (pages 424–425)

4. Is the following sentence true or false? A sea star forces its stomach into the

opening of a clam's shell to digest the clam's body. _____

5. Label the parts of a sea star in the diagram below.

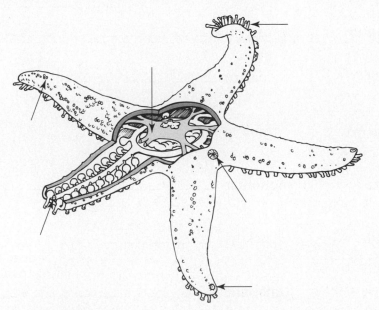

▶ Other Echinoderms (pages 425–426)

6. Complete the table about the characteristics of other echinoderms.

Characteristics of Other Echinoderms			
Characteristics	**Brittle Stars**	**Sand Dollars and Sea Urchins**	**Sea Cucumbers**
Arms			
How they get food			
Movement			

CHAPTER 13, Mollusks, Arthropods, and Echinoderms (continued)

WordWise

Use the clues to help you unscramble the key terms from Chapter 13. Then put the numbered letters in order to find the answer to the riddle.

Clues	Key Terms	
It's a dramatic change in an animal's body.	ashosmtemopri	_ _ _ _ _ _ _ _ _ _ _ _ _ 1
It looks like a small adult.	myphn	_ _ _ _ _ 2
It's a flexible ribbon of teeth.	dalaru	_ _ _ _ _ _ 3
It's shedding an outgrown exoskeleton.	tlnomig	_ _ _ _ _ _ _ 4
It's a mollusk with one shell or none.	sogpotdar	_ _ _ _ _ _ _ _ _ 5
It removes wastes made by cells.	nekdyi	_ _ _ _ _ _ 6
It's the hind section.	omabnde	_ _ _ _ _ _ _ 7
It's protective coloration.	ugalacoefm	_ _ _ _ _ _ _ _ _ _ 8
It's an animal with spiny skin.	nehroicmde	_ _ _ _ _ _ _ _ _ _ 9
It makes up an arthropod's exoskeleton.	tihnci	_ _ _ _ _ _ 10
It's the middle section in insects.	rxaoht	_ _ _ _ _ _ 11
It's on the head and has sense organs.	neantan	_ _ _ _ _ _ _ 12

Riddle: What are the calcium plates that support echinoderms?

Answer: _ _ _ _ _ _ _ _ _ _ _ _
   1 2 3 4 5 6 7 8 9 10 11 12

CHAPTER 14

FISHES, AMPHIBIANS, AND REPTILES

. . . .

SECTION 14-1 ## What Is a Vertebrate?
(pages 432-436)

This section explains how animals with backbones evolved and what their characteristics are.

▶ The Chordate Phylum (pages 432–433)

1. What characteristics do all chordates share? _____

_____

_____

2. A flexible rod that supports an animal's back is called a(n)

_____.

3. Is the following sentence true or false? In vertebrates, part or all of the

notochord is replaced by a backbone. _____

4. What is cartilage? _____

_____

5. Is the following sentence true or false? Pharyngeal slits disappear before

birth in all chordates. _____

▶ The Backbone and Endoskeleton (pages 433–434)

6. The backbone is formed by many similar bones, called _____,
which are lined up in a row.

7. A vertebrate's backbone is part of a(n) _____, or internal
skeleton.

CHAPTER 14, Fishes, Amphibians, and Reptiles *(continued)*

8. Complete the concept map to show the functions of the endoskeleton.

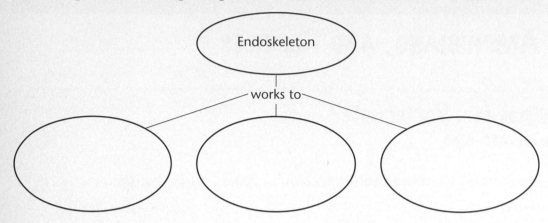

▶ Maintaining Body Temperature (pages 434–435)

9. Circle the letter of each animal that has a body temperature close to the temperature of its environment.

    a. bird   **b.** fish   **c.** reptile   **d.** mammal

10. What is an ectotherm? _____

_____

_____

11. Is the following sentence true or false? A turtle has the same body temperature when it's lying in the sun and when it's swimming in a

    cool river. _____

12. An animal whose body controls and regulates its temperature by

    controlling the internal heat it produces is a(n) _____.

13. Circle the letter of adaptations that help endotherms maintain their body temperature.

    a. spines   **b.** fur   **c.** sweat glands   **d.** cartilage

14. Is the following sentence true or false? Ectotherms can live in a greater

    variety of environments than endotherms can. _____

▶ **Evolution of Vertebrates** (pages 435–436)

15. Circle the letter of the earliest vertebrates.

    a. fishes   **b.** amphibians   **c.** reptiles   **d.** birds

16. What two vertebrates are descended from reptiles? _____

· ·

SECTION 14-2 **Fishes** (pages 437–443)

This section describes the three groups of fishes, how fishes use their gills to get oxygen, and how people use fish.

▶ **Introduction** (page 437)

1. What is a fish? _____

_____

2. Circle the letter of each characteristic of fishes.

    a. gills   **b.** feathers   **c.** scales   **d.** hair

▶ **Obtaining Oxygen** (page 438)

3. Fishes get oxygen from _____.

4. Complete the cycle diagram that shows the path of blood through a fish's circulatory system.

Blood leaves the _____ and enters the gills.

In the gills, the blood gets _____ from the water, while the waste product, _____ moves from the blood into the water.

Oxygen-poor blood moves back to the _____.

Blood moves through _____ to all parts of the body.

© Prentice-Hall, Inc.

CHAPTER 14, Fishes, Amphibians, and Reptiles *(continued)*

▶ Moving and Feeding (page 438)

5. Circle the letter of each sentence that is true about fishes.

   a. Fins help fishes swim by providing a large surface area to push against water.

   b. Fishes that eat insects have sharp, pointed teeth.

   c. Fishes cannot see well in water.

   d. Fishes have keen senses of touch, smell, and taste to help them catch food.

▶ How Fishes Reproduce (page 439)

6. Most fishes have _____ fertilization; the eggs are fertilized outside of the female's body.

7. Is the following sentence true or false? No fishes give birth to live young.

   _____

▶ Fishes Without Jaws (page 439)

8. List the three groups of fishes.

   a. _____ **b.** _____ **c.** _____

9. What two characteristics do biologists use to divide fishes into groups?

   _____

   _____

10. Circle the letter of each sentence that is true about jawless fishes.

    a. Jawless fishes do not have scales.

    b. Jawless fishes have skeletons made of bones.

    c. Jawless fishes have pairs of fins.

    d. Jawless fishes cannot bite.

▶ Cartilaginous Fishes (page 440)

11. The skeletons of cartilaginous fishes are made of _____ .

Science Explorer *Focus on Life Science*

12. Circle the letter of each characteristic of cartilaginous fishes.

    a. jaws   **b.** fins   **c.** scales   **d.** bones

13. Is the following sentence true or false? Cartilaginous fishes are all

herbivores. _____

14. How do sharks' streamlined bodies help them? _____

_____

▶ Bony Fishes (pages 441–442)

Match the parts of bony fishes with their functions. See *Exploring a Bony Fish* on page 441.

Part	Function
_____ **15.** gill cover	**a.** Helps stabilize the fish at different levels in the water
_____ **16.** scales	**b.** Cover the body by overlapping each other
_____ **17.** lateral line	**c.** Sense organ that picks up vibrations and pressure changes in water
_____ **18.** swim bladder	**d.** A flexible flap that opens to release water from the gills

19. What is buoyant force? _____

_____

20. Is the following sentence true or false? If the buoyant force on an object is greater than the weight of the object, then the object floats.

_____

▶ Food for People (page 443)

21. The populations of some fish have been drastically reduced by

_____.

22. Is the following sentence true or false? Raising fish in "fish farms" has increased the demand for fish caught in rivers and oceans.

_____

CHAPTER 14, Fishes, Amphibians, and Reptiles *(continued)*

● ●

SECTION 14-3 Amphibians
(pages 445-450)

This section describes the characteristics of amphibians.

▶ Gills to Lungs (page 446)

1. What is an amphibian? _____

_____

2. Amphibians spend their adulthood on _____, but return

to water to _____.

▶ Amphibian Circulation (page 446)

3. Is the following sentence true or false? Tadpoles have a circulatory

system with two loops. _____

4. Describe the path blood takes in the circulatory system of an adult

amphibian. _____

_____

_____

_____

5. Circle the letter of the two upper chambers of the heart that receive blood.
   a. ventricles   **b.** atria   **c.** vessels   **d.** lungs

6. Is the following sentence true or false? Oxygen-rich blood and oxygen-

poor blood mix in the ventricle. _____

▶ Reproduction and Development (pages 446–447)

7. Is the following sentence true or false? Frogs and salamanders both have
   external fertilization—the eggs are fertilized after the female releases

them. _____

8. Complete the flowchart to show the steps in the metamorphosis of a frog.

Frog Metamorphosis

Fertilized eggs hatch and a legless _____ swims out.

↓

First, _____ legs appear. The skeleton, circulatory system, and digestive system also begin to _____ .

↓

Then the tadpole develops _____ legs. It loses its _____ and starts to breathe with _____ .

↓

The tail is completely gone when the frog is a(n) _____ .

▶ Getting Around on Land (page 448)

9. Circle the letter of each sentence that is true about adaptations for living on land.

a. A land animal must have a strong skeleton to support the body against the pull of gravity.

b. Amphibians were the first vertebrates to have legs.

c. Fish and tadpoles have a transparent membrane to keep their eyes from drying out.

d. Amphibians do not have eyelids.

▶ Frogs and Toads (pages 448–449)

10. How are frogs and toads adapted for hopping and leaping? _____

_____

_____

11. Is the following sentence true or false? Frogs have dry, bumpy skin.

_____

CHAPTER 14, Fishes, Amphibians, and Reptiles *(continued)*

12. List two ways that a frog's coloring is helpful. _____

_____

▶ **Salamanders** (pages 448–449)

13. Amphibians with long, slender bodies that keep their tails as adults are

called _____.

14. How do salamanders get food? _____

_____

15. Is the following sentence true or false? All salamanders live on land as

adults. _____

▶ **Amphibians in Danger** (page 450)

16. The destruction of amphibian _____ is causing
populations of amphibians to decrease.

17. Why are amphibians especially sensitive to changes in the environment?

_____

18. Is the following sentence true or false? The drop in numbers of
amphibians may be a warning that other animals are also in danger.

_____

· ·

SECTION 14-4 **Reptiles**
(pages 451-460)

*This section describes adaptations that enable reptiles to live their entire lives on land.
It also tells about the major groups of reptiles.*

▶ **Protection from Drying Out** (pages 451–453)

1. What is a reptile? _____

_____

2. Circle the letter of the animal that is NOT a reptile.

    a. snake   **b.** alligator   **c.** lizard   **d.** salamander

3. Is the following sentence true or false? Reptiles were the first vertebrates to be well adapted to live their entire lives on land. _____

4. What adaptations does a reptile's egg have to keep it from drying out?

_____

_____

5. What are two functions of a reptile's scaly skin? _____

_____

6. How do the kidneys keep reptiles from losing water? _____

_____

_____

▶ **Obtaining Oxygen from the Air** (page 453)

7. Reptiles get their oxygen from the _____.

8. Is the following sentence true or false? Reptiles have two loops in which their blood circulates through their bodies. _____

9. In lung tissue, _____ moves into the blood and

_____ moves out of the blood.

10. Circle the letter of the number of chambers a reptilian heart has.

    a. two   **b.** three   **c.** four   **d.** five

▶ **Lizards** (pages 453–454)

11. What charactcristics do both lizards and snakes have? _____

_____

_____

_____

CHAPTER 14, Fishes, Amphibians, and Reptiles (continued)

Match each part of a lizard with its function. See *Exploring a Lizard* on page 454.

Part	Function
_____ **12.** crest	**a.** Expands when a male is courting a female or defending his territory
_____ **13.** claws	**b.** Stiffens when a male is making himself look larger
_____ **14.** dewlap	
_____ **15.** nostrils	**c.** Used as a weapon for defense
_____ **16.** tail	**d.** Help a lizard easily climb trees
	e. Help a lizard with its well-developed sense of smell

▶ Snakes (page 455)

17. Circle the letter of each characteristic that snakes have.

    a. no legs   **b.** eyelids   **c.** external ears   **d.** one lung

18. Describe how snakes move. _____

_____

_____

19. Is the following sentence true or false? All snakes are carnivores.

_____

20. Is the following sentence true or false? All snakes have venom glands.

_____

▶ Turtles (page 458)

21. What is a turtle? _____

_____

22. Is the following sentence true or false? All turtles can pull their head,

legs, and tail inside their shell. _____

23. Instead of teeth, turtles have _____ beaks.

▶ Alligators and Crocodiles (page 459)

24. Is the following sentence true or false? Alligators and crocodiles are the

largest living reptiles. _____

25. Complete the Venn diagram to show the similarities and differences
between alligators and crocodiles.

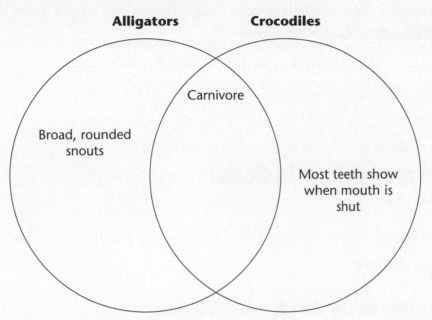

Alligators   **Crocodiles**

Carnivore

Broad, rounded
snouts

Most teeth show
when mouth is
shut

▶ Extinct Reptiles—The Dinosaurs (page 460)

26. Circle the letter of each sentence that is true about dinosaurs.

    a. Reptiles were never the major form of vertebrate life on land.

    b. Dinosaurs might have been endothermic animals.

    c. Dinosaurs were the earliest vertebrates to have legs positioned
    directly under their bodies.

    d. Most carnivorous dinosaurs walked on four legs.

27. What is one theory for the extinction of dinosaurs? _____

_____

_____

_____

28. Some biologists think that _____ are dinosaurs with
feathers.

CHAPTER 14, **Fishes, Amphibians, and Reptiles** *(continued)*

📖 Reading Skill Practice

Writing a summary is one way to review something you have read. Write a summary about the adaptations that reptiles have to live their entire lives on land. You will find this information on pages 451–453. Remember that a summary is much shorter than the reading on which it is based. Do your work on a separate sheet of paper.

SECTION 14–5 **Vertebrate History in Rocks** (pages 461–464)

This section explains how fossils form and how scientists use fossils to infer how living things have changed over time.

▶ Fossils in Sedimentary Rock (pages 462–463)

1. What is a fossil? _____

_____

_____

2. Circle the letter of each sentence that is true about fossils.

   a. Some fossils are imprints in rocks.

   b. Some fossils are the remains of bones or other parts of living things.

   c. Because living tissue decays slowly, many organisms have been preserved as fossils.

   d. Every organism has been preserved as a fossil.

3. Fossils occur most frequently in _____ rock.

4. What are two ways that sediments can build up?

   a. _____

   b. _____

5. Is the following sentence true or false? When the traces of living things are trapped in sediments, they are sometimes preserved as fossils.

_____

▶ Interpretation of Fossils (page 464)

6. Scientists who study extinct organisms, examine fossil structure, and make comparisons to present-day organisms are _____.

7. What can scientists infer from studying fossils? _____

_____

8. Which rock layer in the diagram below is the oldest and which is the youngest?

Oldest layer: _____

Youngest layer: _____

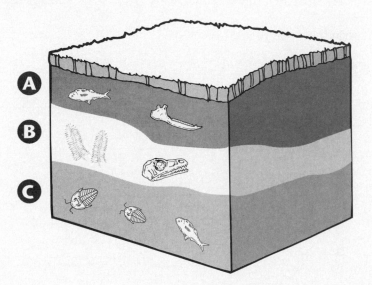

9. What other method do scientists use to determine the age of a fossil?

_____

_____

10. Is the following sentence true or false? As new fossils are found, paleontologists might change their ideas about how different animal groups are related. _____

© Prentice-Hall, Inc.

CHAPTER 14, Fishes, Amphibians, and Reptiles *(continued)*

WordWise

Use the clues to identify the words for the puzzle. Write the words on the lines. Then find the words hidden in the puzzle and circle them. Words are across or up-and-down.

Clues	Key Terms
An animal whose body controls and regulates its temperature	_____
An upper chamber of the heart	_____
The hardened remains of a living thing that existed long ago	_____
An animal that has a notochord, nerve cord, and slits in the throat area	_____
Waste excreted from the body as a watery fluid	_____
A flexible rod that supports an animal's back	_____
The specific environment in which an animal lives	_____
A bone that forms the backbone	_____
An ectothermic vertebrate that lives in water and has fins	_____

```
g  i  d  v  e  r  t  e  b  r  a  n  k  r
e  f  g  w  r  i  s  u  a  h  m  o  f  c
v  o  t  h  a  b  i  t  a  t  y  t  r  h
h  s  v  r  b  h  a  u  e  l  w  o  s  o
l  s  p  f  d  a  t  r  i  u  m  c  y  r
n  i  c  i  f  e  s  a  j  l  i  h  c  d
a  l  i  s  y  u  r  i  n  e  d  o  j  a
q  u  r  h  m  p  k  g  w  s  r  r  b  t
e  n  d  o  t  h  e  r  m  w  o  d  a  e
```

CHAPTER 15

BIRDS AND MAMMALS

SECTION 15-1 Birds (pages 470-479)

This section tells about the characteristics of birds, how they care for their young, and about their special adaptations.

▶ **What Is a Bird?** (page 471)

1. List six characteristics of birds.

   a. _____   b. _____

   c. _____   d. _____

   e. _____   f. _____

2. Is the following sentence true or false? All modern birds evolved from

   ancestors that could not fly. _____

3. Circle the letter of each adaptation that enables birds to fly.

   a. feathers   **b.** hollow bones   **c.** scales   **d.** large chest muscles

▶ **Feathers** (pages 471-472)

Match the bird feathers with their characteristics. Each kind of feather may be used more than once.

Characteristics	Feathers
_____ 4. Traps air to keep bird from losing heat	**a.** contour feather
_____ 5. Balances and steers bird in flight	**b.** down feather
_____ 6. Found right next to a bird's skin	
_____ 7. Gives shape to a bird's body	

CHAPTER 15, Birds and Mammals (continued)

8. Which feather below is a contour feather, and which is a down feather?

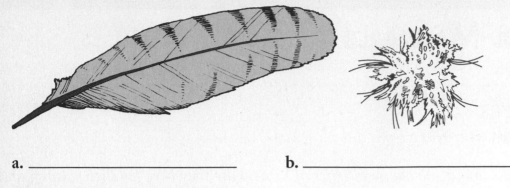

a. _____   b. _____

9. Why do birds preen their feathers? _____

_____

▶ Food and Body Temperature (pages 472–474)

10. Circle the letter of each sentence that is true about birds.

    a. Birds have teeth.

    b. Each bird species has a bill shaped to help it get food quickly and efficiently.

    c. The crop stores food in the body after the bird swallows it.

    d. Chemicals break down food in the gizzard.

11. Small stones help grind food in the _____.

12. Why do birds need a lot of energy? _____

_____

_____

▶ Delivering Oxygen to Cells (pages 475–476)

13. Cells must have enough _____ to release the energy from food.

14. What is the function of air sacs? _____

_____

_____

15. The right side of a bird's heart pumps blood to the _____.

The left side of a bird's heart pumps blood to the _____.

16. What is the advantage of a four-chambered heart? _____

_____

_____

▶ Nervous System and Senses (page 476)

17. Circle the letter of each sentence that is true about the nervous system.

    a. Birds have very quick reactions.

    b. Birds cannot see well.

    c. Birds have a poorly developed brain.

    d. Some birds have a keen sense of hearing.

▶ Reproducing and Caring for Young (pages 476–477)

18. Circle the letter of a characteristic of bird eggs.

    a. soft shell   **b.** leathery shell   **c.** rigid shell   **d.** no shell

19. In most bird species, the female lays the eggs in a(n) _____.

20. How do birds keep their eggs warm so that they will develop? _____

_____

_____

21. How long do parent birds care for their young? _____

_____

_____

▶ Diversity of Birds (pages 477–478)

22. Birds have bills and feet that help them to survive in their

_____.

23. Is the following sentence true or false? A perching bird, such as a

goldfinch, has long legs and toes. _____

CHAPTER 15, Birds and Mammals *(continued)*

24. Ostriches cannot fly. How are they adapted to escape from predators?

_____

_____

▶ Why Birds Are Important (page 479)

25. Circle the letter of each item that birds provide for people.

   a. food   **b.** cotton   **c.** fur   **d.** feathers

26. Is the following sentence true or false? Birds help pollinate flowers and

disperse seeds. _____

27. How do predator birds help people? _____

_____

· ·

SECTION 15–2 The Physics of Bird Flight (pages 480-482)

This section explains how birds fly.

▶ How Air Moves Across a Wing (pages 480–481)

1. Is the following sentence true or false? Gas molecules in air exert

pressure on the objects they surround. _____

2. What causes a balloon to expand when you blow it up? _____

_____

_____

3. Is the following sentence true or false? Moving air exerts more pressure

than air that is not moving. _____

4. The lower surface of a wing is _____ than the upper
surface.

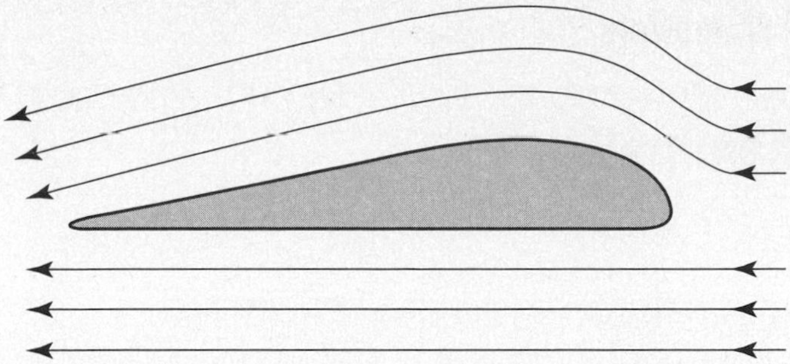

5. Look at the diagram above of a wing. On which side of the wing is air

   moving faster? Explain why. _____

   _____

   _____

6. The air _____ the wing exerts less pressure.

7. What causes lift? _____

   _____

▶ Birds in Flight (pages 481–482)

8. Is the following sentence true or false? Birds get off the ground by

   pushing off with their legs. _____

9. Why do birds pull their wings down when they first take off? _____

   _____

10. Name three different ways that birds can fly.

    a. _____ b. _____ c. _____

11. Which kind of flight requires the most energy? Explain. _____

    _____

    _____

12. Birds rise up into the sky on currents of warm air when

    _____. They coast downward through the air when

    _____.

CHAPTER 15, Birds and Mammals (continued)

• •

SECTION 15–3 **What Is a Mammal?** (pages 483-488)

This section describes the characteristics shared by all mammals.

▶ **Introduction** (pages 483–484)

1. Circle the letter of each characteristic of mammals.

    a. endothermic vertebrate   **b.** feathers

    c. three-chambered heart   **d.** teeth

2. Is the following sentence true or false? The young of most mammals are

    born alive. _____

3. Every young mammal is fed with _____ produced in its

    mother's body.

▶ **Mammals First Appear** (page 484)

4. Circle the letter of each sentence that is true about early mammals.

    a. The ancestors of true mammals were more like birds than mammals.

    b. The earliest mammals were small animals about the size of a mouse.

    c. Early mammals may have been nocturnal, or active at night.

    d. All mammals became specialized to live on land.

▶ **Fur and Hair** (pages 484–485)

5. Is the following sentence true or false? All mammals have fur or hair at

    some point in their lives. _____

6. How do fur and hair help mammals? _____

    _____

    _____

7. Generally, animals in cold regions have _____ coats of fur

    than animals in warmer environments.

▶ Teeth (page 486)

Match the type of teeth with their function. Some functions may be used more than once.

Teeth	Function
_____ **8.** canines	**a.** Bite off and cut parts of food
_____ **9.** molars	**b.** Stab food and tear it
_____ **10.** incisors	**c.** Grind and shred food into tiny bits
_____ **11.** premolars	

12. Look at the teeth in the diagram above. Is this animal an herbivore or a carnivore? How do you know? _____

_____

▶ Getting Oxygen to Cells (page 486)

13. Is the following sentence true or false? All mammals, except whales, breathe with lungs. _____

14. Mammals breathe in and out because of the combined action of rib muscles and a large muscle called the _____ located at the bottom of the chest.

15. Circle the letter of the number of chambers in a mammal's heart.

    a. two   **b.** three   **c.** four   **d.** five

▶ Nervous System and Senses (pages 486–487)

16. What sense do bats use to capture insects? _____

_____

CHAPTER 15, Birds and Mammals (continued)

17. Circle the letter of each sentence that is true about mammals' nervous system.

    a. The brain helps mammals learn, remember, and behave in complex ways.

    b. Squirrels cannot remember what they have learned.

    c. The senses of mammals are adapted for the ways that individual species live.

    d. All mammals can see in color.

▶ Movement (page 487)

18. Most mammals have four _____ and can walk and run.

Match the type of mammal with its specialized way of moving.

Mammal	Way of Moving
_____ 19. bats	a. Have flippers for swimming
_____ 20. dolphins	b. Have wings for flying
_____ 21. gibbons	c. Swing by their arms

▶ Reproducing and Caring for Young (page 488)

22. Circle the letter of the type of fertilization mammals have.

    a. internal   b. external   c. endothermic   d. ectothermic

23. Is the following sentence true or false? Some mammals lay eggs.

    _____

24. All mammals feed their young with milk produced in _____.

📖 Reading Skill Practice

An outline is a good way to organize the information in a section. Write an outline of Section 15–3. Use the headings in the section to organize your outline. Under each heading, write the main idea of that part of the lesson. Then list a few details to support the main idea.

● ●

SECTION 15–4 **Diversity of Mammals**
(pages 491–496)

This section tells about how mammals are classified into different groups.

▶ Introduction (page 491)

1. Complete the concept map to show the groups that mammals are classified into based on how their young develop.

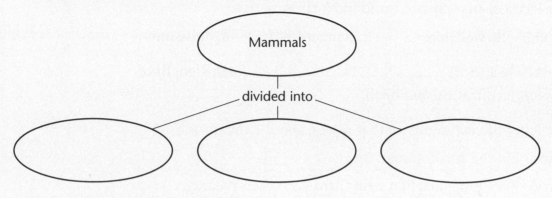

▶ Monotremes (page 492)

2. What are monotremes? _____

_____

Match the monotreme with its characteristics. Some monotremes may be used more than once.

Characteristics	Monotremes
_____ 3. Has sharp spines scattered through hair	**a.** spiny anteater
_____ 4. Lays one to three leathery-shelled eggs into a pouch	**b.** duck-billed platypus
_____ 5. Lays eggs in an underground nest	
_____ 6. Has webbed feet, a bill, and fur	
_____ 7. Eats ants that it digs up with powerful claws	
_____ 8. Lives in the water and constructs a maze of tunnels in the banks	

CHAPTER 15, Birds and Mammals *(continued)*

▶ Marsupials *(pages 492–493)*

9. What are marsupials? _____

   _____

   _____

   _____

10. Circle the letter of marsupials found in North America.

    a. koalas   **b.** wallabies   **c.** kangaroos   **d.** opossums

11. Marsupials have a short _____, the length of
    time between fertilization and birth.

12. Circle the letter of each sentence that is true about kangaroos.

    a. Kangaroos are the smallest marsupials.

    b. Kangaroos have long tails that help them keep their balance.

    c. Female kangaroos give birth to litters of four to five joeys.

    d. Kangaroos are herbivores.

13. The opossum is a(n) _____, it eats fruits, plants, insects,
    and other small animals.

14. How does an opossum protect itself from predators? _____

    _____

    _____

15. Is the following sentence true or false? After being born, young
    opossums crawl into a pouch on their mother's belly and attach to a

    nipple. _____

▶ Placental Mammals *(pages 493–496)*

16. What is a placental mammal? _____

    _____

    _____

17. The organ in pregnant female mammals that passes materials between

the mother and the developing embryo is the _____.

18. Circle the letter of each item that passes from the mother to her young
through the placenta.

   a. wastes   **b.** water   **c.** food   **d.** oxygen

19. What characteristics are used to classify placental mammals into groups?

   a. _____

   b. _____

   c. _____

Match the group of placental mammals with its characteristics. See
Exploring Placental Mammals on pages 494–495.

Placental Mammals

_____ **20.** insect-eaters

_____ **21.** flying mammals

_____ **22.** primates

_____ **23.** rabbits and hares

_____ **24.** rodents

_____ **25.** toothless mammals

_____ **26.** carnivores

_____ **27.** hoofed mammals

_____ **28.** marine mammals

_____ **29.** mammals with trunks

Characteristics

a. Have adaptations for swimming

b. Predators with enlarged canine
teeth

c. Have large brains and opposable
thumbs

d. Gnawing animals with teeth
adapted to grinding food

e. Have forelimbs adapted for flying

f. Have long hind legs specialized
for jumping

g. Have sharp cutting surfaces on all
teeth for eating insects

h. Have long noses adapted for
getting food and water

i. Have small teeth or no teeth at all

j. Have an odd or even number of
toes on the hooves

30. Is the following sentence true or false? The larger the placental

mammal, the shorter its gestation period is. _____

CHAPTER 15, Birds and Mammals *(continued)*

WordWise

Solve the clues by filling in the blanks with key terms from Chapter 15. Then write the numbered letters in the correct order to find the hidden message.

Clues   **Key Terms**

Teeth that grind and shred food   _ _ _ _ _ _
                                        1 2

Material that keeps heat   _ _ _ _ _ _ _ _ _ _
from escaping   3   4

Upward force on a bird's wing   _ _ _ _
                                             5

Helps birds balance and fly   _ _ _ _ _ _   _ _ _ _ _ _ _
                                              6   7

Large muscle that helps   _ _ _ _ _ _ _ _
mammals breathe   8

Pointed teeth that stab and   _ _ _ _ _ _
tear food   9 10

Organ that passes materials   _ _ _ _ _ _ _
between mother and   11   12
developing embryo

Produces milk   _ _ _ _ _ _ _   _ _ _ _ _
                                                 13

Traps heat to keep birds warm   _ _ _ _   _ _ _ _ _ _
                                                    14

Squeezes and grinds food   _ _ _ _ _ _
in a bird's stomach   15

The length of time between   _ _ _ _ _ _ _ _ _   _ _ _ _ _
fertilization and birth   16   17

Hidden Message

_ _ _ _ _ _ _ _ _ _   _ _ _   _ _ _ _ .
1 2 3 4 5 6 7 8 9 10   11 12 13   14 15 16 17

CHAPTER 16

HEALTHY BODY SYSTEMS

How the Body Is Organized (pages 510-515)

This section tells how the body is organized and describes the four types of tissue in the human body.

▶ **Levels of Organization** (pages 510–511)

1. List the levels of organization in the human body, starting with the smallest unit.

    a. _____   b. _____

    c. _____   d. _____

Match the part of the skeletal system with its level of organization. See *Exploring Levels of Organization in the Body* on page 511 in your text.

Parts	Levels of Organization
_____ 2. Thigh bone	**a.** organ system
_____ 3. Living cells widely separated by hard, nonliving material	**b.** organ
_____ 4. Bone cells	**c.** tissue
_____ 5. All the bones, cartilage, and ligaments in body	**d.** cell

▶ **Cells** (page 512)

6. The basic unit of structure and function in a living thing is a(n)

    _____.

7. Circle the letter of the outside boundary of a cell.

    a. cytoplasm   **b.** nucleus   **c.** tissue   **d.** cell membrane

CHAPTER 16, Healthy Body Systems *(continued)*

8. The control center that directs the cell's activities and contains information that determines the cell's characteristics is the

_____.

9. What is the cytoplasm? _____

_____

_____

10. Is the following sentence true or false? Cells carry on the processes that

keep organisms alive. _____

▶ Tissues (pages 512–514)

11. What is a tissue? _____

_____

12. Complete the table to show the functions and examples of the tissues in the human body. See Figure 2 on page 513.

Tissues in the Human Body		
Tissue	**Function**	**Example**
Muscle		
Nerve		
Connective		
Epithelial		

▶ Organs and Organ Systems (pages 514–515)

13. A structure that is made up of different kinds of tissues is a(n)

_____.

14. Circle the letter of the organ.

    a. muscle cell   **b.** blood   **c.** lungs   **d.** digestive system

15. Is the following sentence true or false? An organ has a specific job that is more complex than that of a tissue. _____

16. What is an organ system? _____

_____

_____

Match the organ system with its function. See Figure 4 on page 515.

Organ Systems	Functions
_____ 17. endocrine	**a.** Takes oxygen into the body
_____ 18. circulatory	**b.** Fights disease
_____ 19. excretory	**c.** Removes wastes
_____ 20. respiratory	**d.** Controls body process with chemicals
_____ 21. digestive	**e.** Takes food into the body and breaks it down
_____ 22. immune	**f.** Carries materials to and form body cells

· ·

SECTION 16–2 **Keeping the Body in Balance**
(pages 517–521)

This section describes how the body responds to stress and ways to deal with stress.

▶ **Homeostasis** (pages 518–519)

1. The process by which an organism's internal environment is kept stable in spite of changes in the external environment is called _____.

2. How does your body maintain a constant temperature on a hot day?

_____

_____

_____

CHAPTER 16, Healthy Body Systems *(continued)*

▶ Stress and Homeostasis (pages 519–520)

3. What is stress? _____

_____

4. An event, such as an argument or an upcoming oral report, that causes

stress is a(n) _____.

5. Is the following sentence true or false? Stress does not affect homeostasis.

_____

6. What is adrenaline? _____

_____

7. Complete the flowchart to show the effects of adrenaline on the body.

Adrenaline's Effects

Breathing _____, sending more oxygen to body cells to provide energy for the muscles.

↓

Extra oxygen gets to cells rapidly because the heart beats

_____.

↓

Arms and legs get _____ blood flowing to them.

The skin and digestive system get _____ blood.

↓

The pupils of the eyes get _____, so it is easier to see.

8. What do the reactions of adrenaline prepare the body for? _____

_____

9. Circle the letter of each sentence that is true about the fight-or-flight response.

    a. The fight-or-flight response was important for primitive people who faced wild-animal attacks.

    b. People today do not have the fight-or-flight response.

    c. In the response, the body systems work together to respond to the stressor.

    d. In the response, the respiratory system provides the body with less oxygen.

▶ Long-Term Stress (page 521)

10. Is the following sentence true or false? Even if a stressful situation does not go away, the body can still restore homeostasis. _____

11. What can happen to your body if you do not deal with stress? _____

_____

_____

▶ Dealing With Stress (page 521)

12. Circle the letter of each sentence that is true about dealing with stress.

    a. It is important to ignore stressful situations so that they will go away.

    b. If you accept that you have a problem and deal with it, then your stress will decrease.

    c. Physical activity will only make long-term stress worse.

    d. Talking to people about the stressful situation will help.

Reading Skill Practice

A cycle diagram shows the sequence of events in a continuous process. Make a cycle diagram to show how the body maintains its internal temperature on a very hot day. For more information about cycle diagrams, see page 767 in the Skills Handbook of your textbook. Do your work on a separate sheet of paper.

CHAPTER 16, Healthy Body Systems (continued)

....

| SECTION | **Wellness** |
| 16–3 | (pages 522–526) |

This section explains what wellness is and how to improve your health.

▶ Components of Wellness (pages 522–524)

1. What is wellness? _____

_____

Match each component of wellness with its definition.

Components of Wellness   Definitions

_____ **2.** physical health

_____ **3.** mental health

_____ **4.** social health

a. How you feel about yourself and how you handle daily life demands

b. How well you get along with others

c. How well your body functions

5. Circle the letter of each sentence that is true about the components of wellness.

  a. To be physically healthy, you need to exercise regularly and get enough sleep.

  b. People who are mentally healthy do not feel good about themselves.

  c. Socially healthy people do not have many friends.

  d. Communicating your needs to others is important for social health.

6. Pressure from friends and classmates to behave in certain ways is called

  _____.

▶ Evaluating Your Wellness (page 524)

7. What is a continuum? _____

_____

8. In the illness-wellness continuum in Figure 10 on page 524, the far

  _____ end of the continuum represents perfect wellness.

9. Is the following sentence true or false? Your choices and actions determine where on the continuum your level of health falls.

_____

▶ Improving Your Health (pages 525–526)

10. Circle the letter of how often you must work to improve your wellness.

    a. every day   **b.** once a week   **c.** once a month   **d.** every year

11. List two health-related factors that you cannot change.

    a. _____

    b. _____

12. Circle the letter of each sentence that is true about making decisions.

    a. You make decisions about your health every day.

    b. All the health decisions you make are simple.

    c. Talking to someone is not a good way to make a decision.

    d. Talk to a parent, teacher, or other trusted adult for help with difficult decisions.

13. Complete the flowchart to show the steps in making a healthy decision.

Making a Healthy Decision

Identify the _____.

↓

Outline the _____ and the _____.

↓

Make a(n) _____.

↓

Evaluate the _____.

14. The decision to keep your body healthy is up to _____.

CHAPTER 16, Healthy Body Systems (continued)

WordWise

See how fast you can solve this crossword puzzle. You'll need to use what you've learned about healthy body systems. Go!

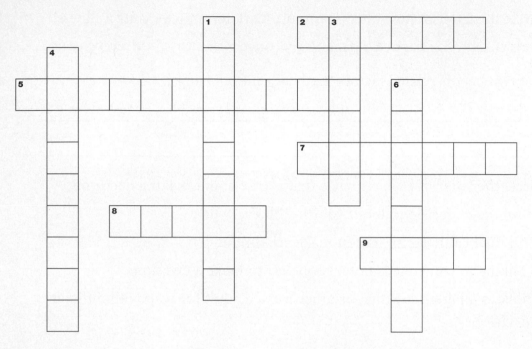

Clues down

1. Jellylike substance between the nucleus and cell membrane

3. A group of similar cells that perform the same function

4. A gradual progression through many stages between two extremes

6. Being at your best possible level of health

Clues across

2. The reaction of your body and mind to threatening events

5. The body's tendency to maintain an internal balance

7. Structure inside the cell that controls the cell's activities

8. A structure made up of different kinds of tissue

9. The basic unit of structure and function in living things.

CHAPTER 17

BONES, MUSCLES, AND SKIN

• •

SECTION 17–1 **The Skeletal System**
(pages 532-539)

This section describes the skeletal system and its function. It also tells how to keep your bones strong and healthy.

▶ What the Skeletal System Does (pages 532–534)

1. List the five major functions of the skeleton.

   a. _____

   b. _____

   c. _____

   d. _____

   e. _____

2. Circle the letter of the bone that makes up the center of the skeleton.
   a. skull   **b.** pelvic girdle   **c.** backbone   **d.** femur

3. The 26 small bones that make up the backbone are the

   _____.

4. How does the skeleton help the body move? _____

   _____

   _____

5. Circle the letter of the bone that protects the brain.
   a. backbone   **b.** pelvic girdle   **c.** ribs   **d.** skull

6. The long bones of the arms and legs make _____.

CHAPTER 17, Bones, Muscles, and Skin *(continued)*

▶ Bones—Strong and Living (pages 534–535)

7. Circle the letter of each sentence that is true about bones.

　a. Bones are very strong and lightweight.

　b. Concrete can absorb more force without breaking than can bone.

　c. Bones make up over half of an adult's body weight.

　d. Bones are hard because they contain minerals.

8. When do bone cells form new bone tissue? _____

_____

_____

▶ The Structure of Bones (pages 535–536)

9. Label the parts of the bone in the diagram below.

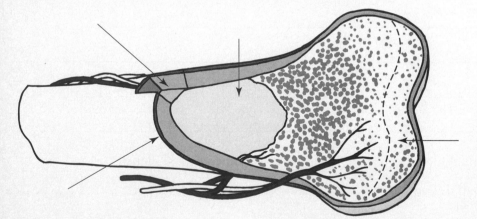

Match each part of a bone with its characteristics.

Bone Parts	Characteristics
_____ **10.** marrow	**a.** Where blood vessels and nerves enter and leave the bone
_____ **11.** outer membrane	**b.** Has small canals with blood vessels running through
_____ **12.** compact bone	**c.** Strong, but lightweight layer because it has many small spaces within it
_____ **13.** spongy bone	**d.** Soft connective tissue in the spaces in bone

　　　　　　　　　Science Explorer Focus on Life Science

▶ How Bones Form (page 536)

14. A connective tissue that is more flexible than bone is called

_____.

15. Circle the letter of each sentence that is true about how bones form.

   a. Much of an infant's skeleton is bone.

   b. As the body grows, the cartilage in the skeleton is replaced with hard bone tissue.

   c. By the time the body stops growing, all of the cartilage has been replaced with bone.

   d. Cartilage covers the ends of many bones in the body of an adult.

▶ Joints of the Skeleton (pages 536–538)

16. What is a joint? _____

_____

17. What are the two kinds of joints in the body?

   a. _____   **b.** _____

18. Circle the letter of the bones that are held together by immovable joints.

   a. knee   **b.** ankle   **c.** ribs   **d.** shoulder blade

19. Complete the table to show the four types of movable joints.

Movable Joints		
Joint	**Kind of Motion**	**Where It's Found in the Body**
Ball-and-socket		
Hinge		
Pivot		
Gliding		

20. The bones in movable joints are held together by a strong connective

tissue called a(n) _____.

CHAPTER 17, Bones, Muscles, and Skin *(continued)*

▶ **Taking Care of Your Bones** (pages 538–539)

21. What can you do to keep your bones healthy? _____

_____

_____

22. A condition in which the body's bones become weak and break easily is

called _____.

Reading Skill Practice

Photographs and illustrations help explain the ideas described in the reading. Look at Figure 4 on page 536. What idea is this photograph communicating? Do your work on a separate sheet of paper.

SECTION 17–2 **The Muscular System**
(pages 540-544)

This section tells about the three kinds of muscle tissue in the human body, how muscles work to move the body, and how to care for your muscles.

▶ **Muscle Action** (page 540)

1. List the two groups of muscles in the body and describe how they are controlled.

a. _____

b. _____

2. Circle the letter of the action that is controlled by involuntary muscles.

    a. smiling   **b.** breathing   **c.** walking   **d.** standing up

▶ Types of Muscles (pages 541–543)

3. Complete the table to compare and contrast the three types of muscle tissue in the body.

Types of Muscles			
Muscles	**Location in Body**	**Voluntary or Involuntary**	**Striated or Not**
Skeletal			
	Inside many internal organs		
Cardiac			

4. A strong connective tissue that attaches muscles to bone is a(n)

_____.

5. The repeated contractions of cardiac muscle are called

_____.

▶ Muscles at Work (page 543)

6. When do muscles contract, or become shorter and thicker? _____

_____

_____

7. Is the following sentence true or false? Muscle cells can extend, or get

longer, as well as contract, or get shorter. _____

8. Why do skeletal muscles work in pairs to move a bone? _____

_____

_____

_____

9. To bend the elbow, the biceps muscle _____ and

the triceps muscle returns to its _____.

CHAPTER 17, Bones, Muscles, and Skin *(continued)*

▶ **Taking Care of Your Skeletal Muscles** (page 544)

10. Circle the letter of the sentence that is true about taking care of muscles.

    a. Exercise makes muscles thicker and stronger.

    b. Warming up muscles before exercise makes muscles more flexible.

    c. Muscles never get injured if you take proper care of them.

    d. Don't rest an injured muscle, it will heal on its own.

···

SECTION 17–3 **Levers in the Body**
(pages 546–549)

This section describes what a lever is and how parts of your body can act like levers.

▶ **Force, Work, and Machines** (page 546)

Match the term with its definition.

Terms	Definitions
_____ **1.** force	**a.** Devices that help you do work
_____ **2.** work	**b.** Done when a force makes an object move
_____ **3.** machines	**c.** A push or a pull on an object

4. When does your body do work? _____

_____

5. List three things that machines change to help do work.

    a. _____

    b. _____

    c. _____

▶ **Levers** (pages 546–547)

6. A rigid object that pivots, or rotates, about a fixed point is called a(n)

_____.

7. Circle the letter of the fixed point around which a lever rotates.

　a. machine 　　　**b.** handle 　　　**c.** lever 　　　**d.** fulcrum

8. The force you exert on a lever is the _____ force. The

　force the lever exerts on an object is the _____ force.

9. What is mechanical advantage? _____

_____

_____

▶ Kinds of Levers (pages 547–548)

10. Classify each of the following levers as first-class, second-class, or third-class.

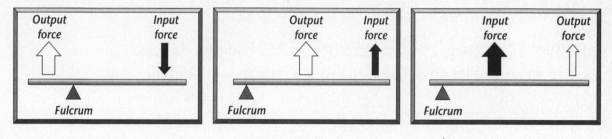

_____ 　　　_____ 　　　_____

Match each lever with its class.

Levers	Classes
_____ **11.** wheelbarrow	**a.** First-class lever
_____ **12.** rake	**b.** Second-class lever
_____ **13.** seesaw	**c.** Third-class lever

▶ Bones and Muscles as Lever Systems (pages 548–549)

14. In the lever system of muscles and bones, a bone is the

　_____, and a joint is the _____.

15. Circle the letter of the part of the body that supplies the input force in a muscle-and-bone lever system.

　a. muscles 　　　**b.** bones 　　　**c.** joints 　　　**d.** tendons

CHAPTER 17, Bones, Muscles, and Skin (continued)

∙∙

SECTION 17–4 **The Skin** (pages 550–556)

This section explains the structure of skin, what skin does, and how to keep skin healthy.

▶ **The Body's Tough Covering** (pages 550–551)

1. Circle the letter of each sentence that is true about the skin.

   a. The skin lets disease-causing microorganisms and harmful substances into the body.

   b. The skin keeps water from escaping from the body.

   c. The skin keeps heat inside the body.

   d. The skin gathers information about the environment.

2. Is the following sentence true or false? To cool the body, blood vessels in the skin enlarge to let more blood run through them to move body heat

   to the outside. _____

3. Why are pain messages important to the body? _____

   _____

   _____

4. Skin cells produce _____ in the presence of sunlight.

▶ **The Epidermis** (pages 552–553)

5. The outermost layer of skin is the _____.

6. Is the following sentence true or false? Nerves and blood vessels run

   through the epidermis. _____

7. New cells that form deep in the epidermis gradually move upward to the

   surface of the skin, where after about _____, the cells die.

8. Is the following sentence true or false? The layer of dead cells on the surface

   of the skin gives the most protection to the body. _____

9. Is the following sentence true or false? Melanin, a pigment that gives skin its color, protects the skin from burning in sunlight. _____

▶ The Dermis (page 553)

10. The lower layer of the skin is the _____.

11. Circle the letter of each structure in the dermis.

    a. hairs   **b.** bones   **c.** sweat glands   **d.** oil glands

12. Perspiration reaches the surface of the skin through openings called

    _____.

13. What are follicles? _____

_____

▶ Caring for Your Skin (pages 554–556)

14. Complete the concept map to show how to keep your skin healthy.

15. What should you do to replace the water that the skin loses during

    perspiration? _____

_____

16. What is acne? _____

_____

CHAPTER 17, Bones, Muscles, and Skin (continued)

WordWise

Use the clues below to identify key terms from Chapter 17. Write the terms on the line, putting one letter in each blank. When you finish, the word enclosed in the diagonal lines will reveal the name of the outermost layer of skin.

Clues

1. A rigid object that pivots, or rotates, about a fixed point

2. An opening in the dermis through which perspiration reaches the surface of the skin

3. A place in the body where two bones come together

4. A strong connective tissue that attaches muscle to bone

5. A push or pull on an object

6. A soft connective tissue found in the spaces in bone

7. The fixed point around which a lever rotates

8. A connective tissue that makes up the skeleton that is more flexible than bone

9. Muscles attached to the bones of the skeleton are _____ muscles.

Key Terms

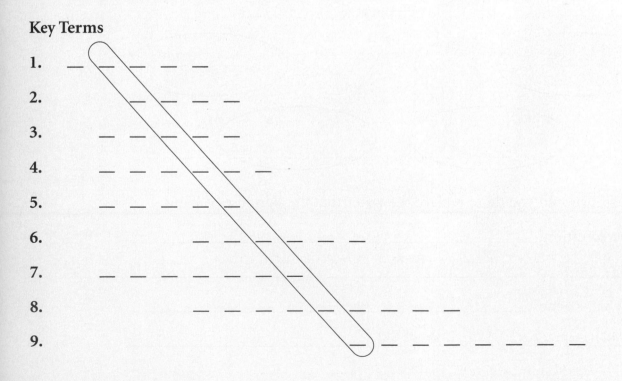

1. __ __ __ __ __

2. __ __ __ __

3. __ __ __ __

4. __ __ __ __ __ __

5. __ __ __ __ __

6. __ __ __ __ __

7. __ __ __ __ __ __

8. __ __ __ __ __ __ __ __

9. __ __ __ __ __ __ __

Science Explorer *Focus on Life Science*

CHAPTER 18

FOOD AND DIGESTION

....

SECTION 18-1 **Food and Energy**
(pages 562-569)

This section tells about the six nutrients needed by the body.

▶ Why You Need Food (pages 562–563)

1. What two things does food give to your body?

   a. _____

   b. _____

2. Is the following sentence true or false? Food is required for the body to

   maintain homeostasis, keeping a steady internal state. _____

3. The substances in food that give the raw materials and the energy

   needed by the body are called _____.

4. List the six kinds of nutrients that people need to stay healthy.

   a. _____   b. _____   c. _____

   d. _____   e. _____   f. _____

5. The amount of energy released by nutrients in the body is measured in

   units called _____.

6. Is the following sentence true or false? The more active you are, the more

   Calories you need. _____

▶ Carbohydrates (pages 563–564)

7. Carbohydrates are a major source of _____.

CHAPTER 18, Food and Digestion *(continued)*

8. Is the following sentence true or false? Carbohydrates are not needed

    for making new body cells. _____

Match the foods with the kinds of carbohydrates. Each kind of
carbohydrate may be used more than once.

Foods	Kinds of Carbohydrates
_____ **9.** fiber	**a.** Simple carbohydrate
_____ **10.** glucose	**b.** Complex carbohydrate
_____ **11.** starch	
_____ **12.** sugar	

▶ Fats (page 565)

13. What are fats? _____

    _____

14. Circle the letter of the nutrient that provides the most energy.

    a. glucose   **b.** fats   **c.** carbohydrates   **d.** vitamins

15. List three jobs that fats have in the body.

    a. _____

    b. _____

    c. _____

16. Complete the following table to compare the two kinds of fats.

Kinds of Fats		
Characteristics	**Unsaturated Fats**	**Saturated Fats**
Liquid or Solid		
Foods Found In		

▶ Proteins (page 566)

17. Nutrients that contain nitrogen, as well as carbon, hydrogen, and oxygen are called _____.

18. List three ways in which proteins are used by the body.

a. _____

b. _____

c. _____

19. Circle the letter of the food that contains high amounts of proteins.

    a. sugar   **b.** fiber   **c.** olive oil   **d.** beans

20. Is the following sentence true or false? The body can make all of the amino acids it needs to make proteins. _____

Match the kind of protein with its characteristics. Each kind of characteristic may be used more than once.

Characteristics	Kinds of Proteins
_____ **21.** Missing one or more essential amino acids	**a.** complete protein
_____ **22.** Contains all the essential amino acids	**b.** incomplete protein
_____ **23.** Comes from animal sources, such as meat and eggs	
_____ **24.** Comes from plant sources, such as grains and nuts	

▶ Vitamins (pages 566–568)

25. What are vitamins? _____

_____

26. Circle the letter of each sentence that is true about vitamins.

    a. The body needs large amounts of vitamins.

    b. Most people get the vitamins they need from foods.

    c. If you eat a variety of foods, you will get enough of each vitamin.

    d. Fat-soluble vitamins are stored in fatty tissues in the body.

CHAPTER 18, Food and Digestion (continued)

▶ **Minerals** (pages 568–569)

27. Nutrients that are not made by living things are called

_____.

28. How do you get minerals into your diet? _____

_____

Match the mineral with its function. See Figure 6 on page 568.

Minerals	Functions
_____ **29.** iron	**a.** Needed for normal muscle and nerve function
_____ **30.** fluorine	**b.** Helps maintain water balance
_____ **31.** magnesium	**c.** Forms an important part of red blood cells
_____ **32.** potassium	**d.** Helps form bones and teeth

▶ **Water** (page 569)

33. The most abundant substance in the body is _____.

34. Why is water the body's most important nutrient? _____

_____

_____

· ·

SECTION 18-2 **Healthy Eating**
(pages 571-575)

This section describes the Food Guide Pyramid and how to read labels on foods.

▶ **The Food Guide Pyramid** (pages 572–573)

1. How does the Food Guide Pyramid help you plan a healthy diet?

_____

_____

2. Which foods in the pyramid should make up the largest part of the diet?

_____

_____

_____

3. Foods in the Fats, Oils, and Sweets group should be used

_____ .

▶ Food Labels (pages 572–575)

4. Is the following sentence true or false? All foods except meat, poultry, fresh vegetables, and fresh fruit must be labeled with nutrition

information. _____

5. The information on the food label, such as the number of Calories and

the nutrient content, is based on the _____ .

6. What does it mean when a food label shows that Calories is equal to 110?

_____

_____

7. What is the Percent Daily Value on a food label? _____

_____

_____

8. Is the following sentence true or false? All people have the same daily

requirements for nutrients and Calories. _____

9. The food label lists the ingredients in the food in order by

_____ , starting with the main ingredient.

10. Why is it helpful to read the list of ingredients? _____

_____

_____

CHAPTER 18, Food and Digestion *(continued)*

....

SECTION 18-3
The Digestive Process Begins
(pages 576-581)

This section explains what the digestive system does and describes the functions of the mouth, the throat, and the stomach.

▶ Functions of the Digestive System (pages 576–577)

1. Complete the flowchart to show the role of the digestive system.

Digestive System

The digestive system breaks down _____ into molecules the body can use.

↓

Then, molecules are absorbed into the _____ and carried throughout the body.

↓

Finally, the digestive system removes _____ from the body.

2. What is digestion? _____

_____

3. Is the following sentence true or false? In chemical digestion, foods are physically broken down into smaller pieces by chewing.

_____

4. The process by which nutrient molecules pass through the wall of the

digestive system and into the blood is called _____.

5. What happens to materials that are not absorbed? _____

_____

Science Explorer *Focus on Life Science*

▶ The Mouth (page 578)

6. The fluid released when your mouth waters is called _____.

7. Circle the letter of the object that begins the process of mechanical digestion in the mouth.

    a. saliva   **b.** teeth   **c.** enzymes   **d.** mucus

8. What occurs during chemical digestion in the mouth? _____

_____

_____

▶ The Esophagus (page 579)

Match each term with its definition.

Terms	Definitions
_____ **9.** epiglottis	**a.** A thick, slippery substance that makes food easier to swallow
_____ **10.** esophagus	**b.** A flap of tissue that seals off the windpipe, preventing food from entering it
_____ **11.** mucus	**c.** A muscular tube that connects the mouth to the stomach
_____ **12.** peristalsis	**d.** Involuntary waves of muscle contraction that push food through the digestive system

▶ The Stomach (pages 580–581)

13. Circle the letter of each sentence that is true about the stomach.

    a. The stomach is a J-shaped muscular pouch in the abdomen.

    b. Mechanical digestion does not occur in the stomach.

    c. Digestive juice in the stomach contains an enzyme that breaks down proteins.

    d. Hydrochloric acid in the stomach kills many bacteria that are swallowed with food.

CHAPTER 18, Food and Digestion *(continued)*

14. Give two reasons why the hydrochloric acid in the digestive juice does not damage the stomach.

a. _____

b. _____

📖 Reading Skill Practice

Using the glossary is a quick way to look up the meanings of key terms in the textbook. The glossary is located in the back of your textbook, beginning on page 776. Make a list of the key terms in this section. Then use the glossary to write the definition for each. Do your work on a separate sheet of paper.

SECTION 18-4 **Final Digestion and Absorption**
(pages 584–587)

This section describes the roles of the small and large intestines in digestion.

▶ **The Small Intestine** (pages 584–587)

1. What takes place in the small intestine? _____

_____

2. List the three organs that produce the enzymes and secretions used in the small intestine.

a. _____ b. _____ c. _____

3. The largest and heaviest organ inside the body that is located in the

upper part of the abdomen is the _____.

4. A triangular organ that lies between the stomach and the first part of

the small intestine is called the _____.

5. Enzymes produced by the pancreas help break down

_____, _____, and _____.

6. What is the role of fiber? _____

_____

_____

7. The tiny finger-shaped structures that cover the inner surface of the

small intestine are called _____.

8. Is the following sentence true or false? Nutrient molecules pass from
the small intestine into the bloodstream through the villi.

_____

▶ The Large Intestine (page 587)

9. Is the following sentence true or false? The bacteria in the large
intestine feed on the material passing through and make certain

vitamins for the body. _____

10. Complete the concept map to show the role of the large intestine.

11. The short tube at the end of the large intestine where waste material is

compressed is called the _____.

12. Circle the letter of the muscular opening through which wastes are
removed from the body.

a. rectum   **b.** anus   **c.** pancreas   **d.** villi

CHAPTER 18, Food and Digestion *(continued)*

WordWise

Answer the questions by writing the correct key term in the blanks. Use the circled letter in each term to find the hidden key term. Then write a definition for the hidden key term.

1. What is the triangular organ that lies between the stomach and the first part of the small intestine and produces enzymes that help break down starches, proteins, and fats?

 _ _ ⃝ _ _ _ _ _

2. What is a thick, slippery substance produced by the body that makes food move more easily through the digestive system?

 _ _ _ ⃝ _

3. What nutrient acts as a helper molecule in many different chemical reactions within the body?

 _ _ ⃝ _ _ _ _ _

4. What is the process by which nutrient molecules pass through the wall of the digestive system into the blood?

 _ _ _ _ ⃝ _ _ _ _ _

5. What was developed by nutritionists to classify foods into six major groups and tell how many servings from each group to eat?

 _ _ _ _ _ _ ⃝ _ _ _ _ _ _ _ _ _

6. What is the organ that stores bile until it is needed in the small intestine?

 _ _ _ _ _ _ _ _ _ _ ⃝ _

7. What is a protein that speeds up chemical reactions in the body?

 _ ⃝ _ _ _ _

8. What is a fat that is usually solid at room temperature and is found in meat, dairy products, and egg yolks?

 _ _ ⃝ _ _ _ _ _ _ _ _ _

Key Term: _ _ _ _ _ _ _ _

Definition: _____

_____

CHAPTER 19

CIRCULATION

. . . .

SECTION 19–1 ## The Body's Transportation System
(pages 594-600)

This section describes how the heart, blood vessels, and blood work together to carry materials throughout the body.

▶ Movement of Materials (pages 594–595)

1. Another name for the cardiovascular system is the _____ system.

2. Complete this concept map to show what makes up the cardiovascular system.

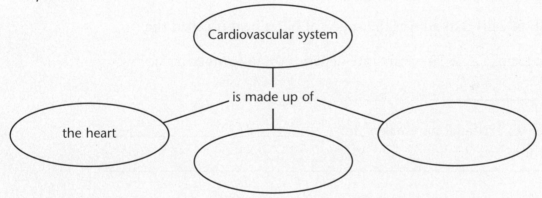

3. What three things are carried throughout the body by the cardiovascular

   system? _____

   _____

▶ The Heart (pages 596–597)

4. Each time the heart beats, what does it do to blood? _____

   _____

   _____

CHAPTER 19, Circulation *(continued)*

5. Complete the table about the chambers of the heart.

Chambers of the Heart		
Questions	Upper Chambers	Lower Chambers
What are these chambers called?		
How many are there?		
What is the function, or job, of these chambers?		

6. A flap of tissue that prevents blood from flowing backward is a(n)

_____.

▶ Regulation of Heartbeat (page 598)

7. The group of cells that adjusts the speed of heart beat is called the

_____. The heart rate depends on how much

_____ the body needs.

8. What does an artificial pacemaker do? _____

_____

9. Name the three kinds of blood vessels. _____

_____

▶ Two Loops (pages 598-600)

10. Describe the loop in which the blood picks up oxygen. _____

_____

_____

_____

11. Draw arrows on the diagram at the right to show how blood circulates through the body. The first arrow should start in the right ventricle.

12. The largest artery in the body is call

the _____.

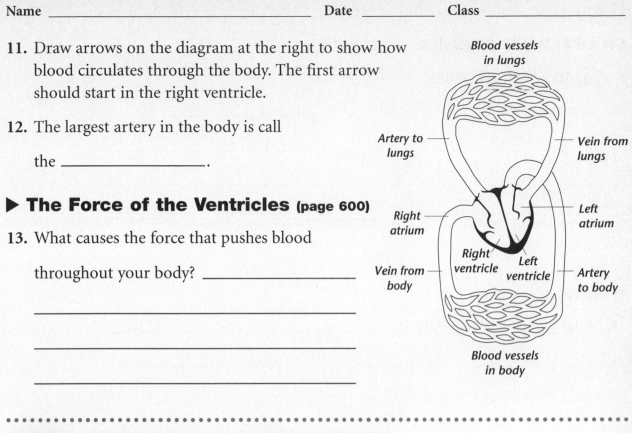

Blood vessels in lungs

Artery to lungs

Vein from lungs

Right atrium

Left atrium

Right ventricle

Left ventricle

Vein from body

Artery to body

Blood vessels in body

▶ The Force of the Ventricles (page 600)

13. What causes the force that pushes blood

throughout your body? _____

_____

_____

_____

. . . .

SECTION 19-2 A Closer Look at Blood Vessels
(pages 601-605)

This section describes three kinds of blood vessels that are found in your body.

▶ Arteries (pages 601–603)

1. Arteries carry blood away from the _____.

2. Is the following sentence true or false? The coronary arteries provide

the stomach with its blood supply. _____

3. Circle the letter of each sentence that is true about pulse.

   a. The faster your heart beats, the slower your pulse will be.

   b. Pulse is caused by the expanding and narrowing of artery walls.

   c. When you count pulse beats, you are also counting heartbeats.

   d. You can feel pulse in veins but not in arteries.

4. Is the following sentence true or false? Arteries control the amount of

blood that different organs receive. _____

CHAPTER 19, Circulation *(continued)*

▶ Capillaries (page 603)

5. What important thing happens in the capillaries? _____

_____

_____

6. One process in which materials are exchanged between the blood and the

body cells is _____.

▶ Veins (page 604)

7. What job do veins carry out? _____

_____

8. What three things help push blood through veins?

a. _____

b. _____

c. _____

▶ Blood Pressure (pages 604–605)

9. What is blood pressure? _____

_____

10. Circle the letter of the name of the instrument that measures blood pressure.

a. stethoscope   b. X-ray machine   c. sphygmomanometer   d. mercury

---

📖 **Reading Skill Practice**

By looking carefully at photographs and illustrations in textbooks, you can help yourself understand what you have read. Look carefully at Figure 9 on page 604. What important idea does this photograph communicate?

Science Explorer *Focus on Life Science*

SECTION 19-3 Blood and Lymph (pages 607-612)

This section explains what blood is made of and describes the jobs performed by the different parts of blood. This section also describes the lymphatic system.

▶ Introduction (page 607)

1. What is the name for the liquid part of blood? _____

2. Complete the concept map below by naming the types of cells that are found in blood.

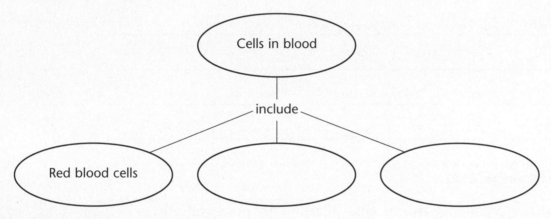

▶ Plasma (page 607)

3. What is plasma mostly made up of? _____

4. List four kinds of materials that are carried in plasma.

a. _____

b. _____

c. _____

d. _____

▶ Red Blood Cells (pages 608–609)

5. What job do red blood cells perform in the body? _____

_____

_____

CHAPTER 19, Circulation *(continued)*

6. What is hemoglobin, and where is it found? _____

_____

_____

_____

▶ White Blood Cells (page 609)

7. What is the job of white blood cells? _____

8. List four ways in which white blood cells are different from red blood cells.

a. _____

b. _____

c. _____

d. _____

▶ Platelets (page 610)

9. Is the following sentence true or false? Platelets are pieces of cells.

_____

10. Describe how a blood clot forms. _____

_____

_____

▶ Blood Types (pages 610–611)

Match the blood type with the kinds of clumping proteins in its plasma.

Blood Type	Clumping Proteins in Its Plasma
_____ **11.** A	**a.** no clumping proteins
_____ **12.** B	**b.** anti-B proteins
_____ **13.** AB	**c.** both anti-A and anti-B proteins
_____ **14.** O	**d.** anti-A proteins

15. What is a blood transfusion? _____

_____

16. Why can't a person with blood type A safely receive a transfusion of

blood type B? _____

_____

_____

▶ The Lymphatic System (page 612)

17. The fluid inside the lymphatic system is called _____.

18. What is the lymphatic system? _____

_____

_____

19. How do lymph nodes help fight disease? _____

_____

_____

| SECTION 19-4 | **Cardiovascular Health** (pages 614–618) |

This section describes diseases of the cardiovascular system. The section also identifies steps that people can take to help prevent these diseases.

▶ Cardiovascular Disease (page 615)

1. What is atherosclerosis? _____

_____

_____

2. What is cholesterol? _____

_____

CHAPTER 19, Circulation *(continued)*

3. Complete the flowchart below, which describes what can happen when atherosclerosis develops in the coronary arteries.

Atherosclerosis

Atherosclerosis develops in coronary arteries.

↓

Heart muscle receives less _____, and therefore its cells receive less _____.

↓

A(n) _____ occurs, which means that blood flow to part of the heart is cut off.

▶ Hypertension (pages 615–617)

4. What is hypertension? _____

_____

_____

5. Give two reasons why hypertension is a serious problem. _____

_____

_____

_____

6. What is done to treat hypertension? _____

_____

_____

▶ Keeping Your Cardiovascular System Healthy (page 618)

7. To help maintain cardiovascular health, people should eat a diet that is low in these substances.

a. _____

b. _____

c. _____

8. Is the following sentence true or false? Even if smokers quit, they cannot decrease their risk of death from cardiovascular disease. _____

9. In the table below, explain why each behavior is important for cardiovascular health.

Cardiovascular Health	
Behavior	**Why It Is Important**
Getting a lot of exercise	
Eating healthy foods	
Not smoking	

 **Reading Skill Practice**

Outlining is a way to help yourself understand and remember what you have read. Write an outline of this section on cardiovascular health. In an outline, copy the headings in the textbook. Under each heading, write the main idea of that part of the lesson. Then list the details that support that main idea.

CHAPTER 19, Circulation *(continued)*

Word Wise

See how fast you can solve this crossword puzzle. You'll need to use what you've learned about the cardiovasculary system. Go!

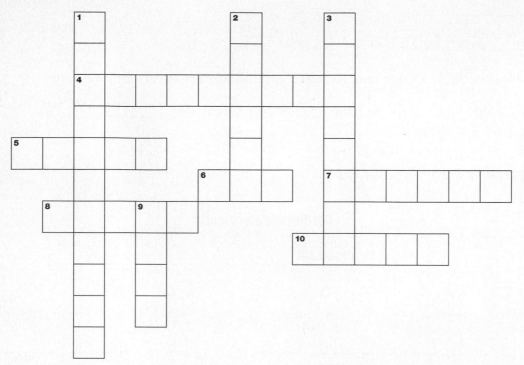

Clues down

1. Tiny blood vessels in which substances are exchanged between the blood and body cells

2. The liquid part of blood

3. The kind of artery that supplies blood to the heart itself

9. A blood vessel that carries blood back to the heart

Clues across

4. A group of cells located in the right atrium that regulates heartbeat rate

5. The alternating expansion and contraction of artery walls caused by the contraction and relaxation of the ventricles; can be felt if you touch your wrist

6. To keep your heart healthy, you should limit this in the food you eat.

7. A chamber of the heart that receives blood that comes into the heart

8. A flap of tissue that prevents blood from flowing backward

10. The fluid that the lymphatic system collects and returns to the bloodstream

Science Explorer Focus on Life Science

CHAPTER 20

RESPIRATION AND EXCRETION

SECTION 20-1 The Respiratory System
(pages 624-632)

This section describes the parts of the respiratory system and how they work to help you breathe and speak.

▶ **Introduction** (page 624)

1. What are two functions of the respiratory system?

   a. _____

   b. _____

▶ **Why the Body Needs Oxygen** (pages 624–625)

2. The chemical reactions to release energy that take place inside your cells

   must have _____.

3. What is respiration? _____

   _____

   _____

4. List three products of respiration.

   a. _____   b. _____   c. _____

5. Is the following sentence true or false? To a scientist, *breathing* and

   respiration mean the same thing. _____

6. Circle the letter of each organ system that the respiratory system depends on.

   a. circulatory system   **b.** reproductive system

   c. excretory system   **d.** digestive system

CHAPTER 20, Respiration and Excretion *(continued)*

▶ The Air You Breathe (page 625)

7. Circle the letter of each sentence that is true about oxygen.

   a. The air you breathe is part of the Earth's atmosphere, the blanket of gases that surrounds Earth.

   b. Oxygen makes up about 78 percent of the gases in the atmosphere.

   c. Your body uses all of the air that you breathe into your lungs.

   d. Most of the air you breathe in goes back into the atmosphere when you exhale.

▶ The Path of Air (pages 626–628)

8. Is the following sentence true or false? When you breathe in air, you

   also breathe in dust, pollen, and microorganisms. _____

9. Complete the flowchart to show the path of air as it travels to the lungs.

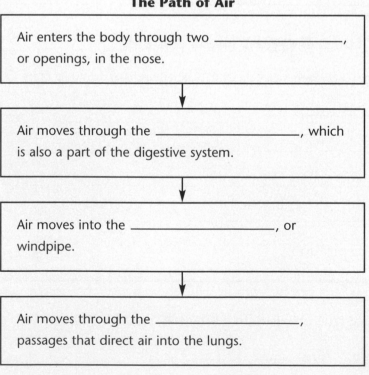

The Path of Air

Air enters the body through two _____, or openings, in the nose.

Air moves through the _____, which is also a part of the digestive system.

Air moves into the _____, or windpipe.

Air moves through the _____, passages that direct air into the lungs.

10. What does a sneeze do? _____

    _____

11. Another name for the pharynx is the _____.

Science Explorer Focus on Life Science

Match the parts of the nose with their functions.

Parts	Functions
_____ **12.** nostrils	**a.** Moistens the air and traps particles in the air
_____ **13.** nasal cavities	**b.** Openings in the nose through which air enters
_____ **14.** mucus	**c.** Tiny hairlike extensions that sweep mucus into the throat
_____ **15.** cilia	**d.** Contain blood vessels that heat the air you breathe in

16. Circle the letter of each body part that is connected to the pharynx.

a. stomach   **b.** nose   **c.** mouth   **d.** ears

17. The walls of the trachea are made up of rings of _____ that strengthen the trachea and keep it open.

18. Is the following sentence true or false? The cilia and mucus in the trachea sweep upward, moving the mucus toward the nose where it is

sneezed out. _____

19. If food enters the trachea, a person can _____.

20. Circle the letter of the main organs of the respiratory system.

a. trachea   **b.** bronchi   **c.** lungs   **d.** alveoli

21. Is the following sentence true or false? Inside the lungs, each bronchus

divides into smaller and smaller tubes. _____

22. What happens in the alveoli? _____

_____

▶ **Gas Exchange** (page 629)

23. What occurs during the process of gas exchange? _____

_____

_____

CHAPTER 20, Respiration and Excretion *(continued)*

24. Why can the lungs absorb a large amount of oxygen? _____

_____

_____

▶ How You Breathe (pages 630–631)

25. Is the following sentence true or false? The more oxygen you need, the

more slowly you breathe. _____

26. What is the diaphragm? _____

_____

27. Complete the cycle diagram to show the process of breathing.

Rib muscles and diaphragm contract, making

the chest cavity _____.

The air is squeezed out of the

_____, and you exhale.

The pressure of the air inside the lungs

_____.

The rib muscles and diaphragm relax, and the

chest cavity becomes _____.

Air rushes into the lungs, and you

_____.

▶ How You Speak (pages 631–632)

28. Another name for the voice box is the _____.

29. What are vocal cords? _____

_____

_____

30. How do vocal cords create your voice? _____

_____

_____

_____

📖 Reading Skill Practice

Taking notes while you read is a very helpful way to remember what you have read. To take notes, write down the headings in the section. Under each heading, write the main idea and important details that you read about. You should also include the key terms and their definitions in your notes. Reread this section. As you read, take notes about what you are reading. Do your work on a separate sheet of paper.

© Prentice-Hall, Inc.

SECTION 20-2 **Smoking and Your Health**
(pages 634–638)

This section explains what harmful chemicals are in tobacco smoke and how these chemicals harm the body.

▶ Chemicals in Tobacco Smoke (pages 634–635)

1. Complete the table to show the harmful chemicals in tobacco smoke.

Harmful Chemicals in Tobacco Smoke		
Chemical	**What It Is**	**How It Harms the Body**
Tar		
Carbon monoxide		
	A drug that produces an addiction, or physical dependence	

CHAPTER 20, Respiration and Excretion (continued)

▶ Respiratory System Problems (pages 635–636)

2. Circle the letter of each sentence that is true about the effects of tobacco smoke.

   a. Tobacco smoke does not harm the respiratory system.

   b. Smokers cough frequently because their cilia cannot sweep away mucus.

   c. Smokers do not get as much oxygen because mucus buildup blocks air flow into the lungs.

   d. Heavy smokers can easily take part in vigorous sports.

3. List three respiratory problems that result from long-term smoking.

   a. _____ **b.** _____ **c.** _____

4. Is the following sentence true or false? Long-term bronchitis has no

   effect on the breathing passages. _____

5. A serious disease that destroys lung tissue and causes difficulty in

   breathing is _____.

6. What causes emphysema? _____

   _____

   _____

7. Is the following sentence true or false? Cigarette smoke has over 40

   different chemicals that cause cancer. _____

▶ Circulatory System Problems (page 637)

8. How do the chemicals in tobacco smoke affect blood vessels?

   _____

   _____

   _____

   _____

9. Is the following sentence true or false? Smokers are more likely to have

heart attacks than nonsmokers. _____

▶ Passive Smoking (page 637)

10. What is passive smoking? _____

_____

_____

11. Is the following sentence true or false? Passive smoking causes
respiratory problems and increases the risk of heart disease and lung

cancer in nonsmokers. _____

▶ Choosing Not to Smoke (page 638)

12. Most smokers began smoking when they were _____.

13. List two reasons why people are tempted to start smoking.

a. _____

b. _____

14. Is the following sentence true or false? It is very easy to stop smoking

once you have started. _____

· ·

SECTION 20-3 The Excretory System
(pages 639-644)

This section explains how the parts of the excretory system work.

▶ Introduction (page 639)

1. What is the function of the excretory system? _____

_____

_____

_____

CHAPTER 20, Respiration and Excretion *(continued)*

2. The process of removing wastes from the body is _____.

▶ The Kidneys (pages 639–640)

3. What are three wastes that the body must get rid of? _____

_____

Match the term with its definition.

Terms	Definitions
_____ **4.** urea	**a.** The major organs of the excretory system
_____ **5.** kidneys	**b.** A watery fluid produced by the kidneys
_____ **6.** urine	**c.** A chemical that comes from the breakdown of proteins

7. Complete the flowchart to show how wastes are removed from the body.

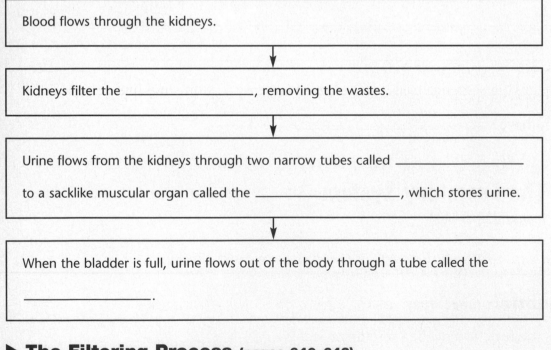

Removing Wastes

Blood flows through the kidneys.

Kidneys filter the _____, removing the wastes.

Urine flows from the kidneys through two narrow tubes called _____ to a sacklike muscular organ called the _____, which stores urine.

When the bladder is full, urine flows out of the body through a tube called the _____.

▶ The Filtering Process (pages 640–642)

8. What are nephrons? _____

_____

_____

9. What are the stages of urine formation?

a. _____

b. _____

10. Is the following sentence true or false? Urea and glucose stay in the capillaries while blood cells and protein molecules move into the capsule of a nephron. _____

11. List the substances that are returned to the blood and those that stay in the kidneys after the kidneys filter the blood.

Returned to blood: _____

Stay in kidneys: _____

12. Why is a chemical analysis of urine useful to doctors? _____

_____

_____

_____

▶ Water Balance in the Body (pages 643–644)

13. The kidneys help maintain homeostasis by regulating the amount of

_____ in the body.

14. Is the following sentence true or false? If you've been sweating a lot and haven't had much to drink, your body will absorb less water and produce a larger volume of urine. _____

▶ Other Organs of Excretion (page 644)

15. What are three other organs of excretion, not including the kidneys?

a. _____ b. _____ c. _____

16. What is the function of the liver? _____

_____

_____

CHAPTER 20, Respiration and Excretion (continued)

WordWise

Use the clues to help you unscramble the key terms from Chapter 20. Then put the numbered letters in order to find the answer to the riddle.

Clues	Key Terms
It's the result of proteins breaking down.	euar — — — — 　　　　1
It's tiny sacs of lung tissue.	vlelioa — — — — — — — 　　　　　　2
It's an irritation of the breathing passages.	crtoibnsih — — — — — — — — — — 　　　　　　　　　　3
It's a tiny filtering factory in the kidneys.	renhnop — — — — — — — 　　　　　4
It's a large muscle that helps you breathe.	gahmdairp — — — — — — — — — 　　　　5
It's a small tube through which urine leaves the body.	reahrut — — — — — — — 　　　　6
It's the voice box.	yranxl — — — — — — 　　　　7
It's a dark substance and makes cilia clump together.	rta — — — 　8
They're tiny, hairlike, and sweep mucus around.	alici — — — — — 　　　　9
It's a dangerous chemical in tobacco smoke.	tnocinei — — — — — — — — 　　　　　10
It's the major organ of the excretory system.	ydnkie — — — — — — 　　　　11

Riddle: What process releases energy from oxygen and glucose?

Answer: — — — — — — — — — — —
　　　　　1　2　3　4　5　6　7　8　9　10　11

CHAPTER 21

FIGHTING DISEASES

···

SECTION 21–1 ## Infectious Disease
(pages 650-654)

This section explains how infectious diseases are caused and what kinds of organisms cause disease.

▶ Disease and Pathogens (page 651)

1. Organisms that cause disease are called _____.

2. What is an infectious disease? _____

_____

_____

3. Is the following sentence true or false? Pathogens make you sick by

   damaging individual cells. _____

▶ Understanding Infectious Disease (page 651)

4. Circle the letter of each sentence that is true about infectious disease.

   a. People always knew that organisms could cause disease.

   b. People once thought evil spirits or swamp air made people sick.

   c. Louis Pasteur showed that killing microorganisms could stop the
   spread of disease.

   d. Each infectious disease is caused by many different pathogens.

▶ Kinds of Pathogens (pages 652–653)

5. Is the following sentence true or false? Most diseases are caused by

   pathogens that are very large. _____

CHAPTER 21, Fighting Diseases *(continued)*

6. Complete the concept map to show the different kinds of pathogens.

7. In what two ways do bacteria cause disease?

a. _____

b. _____

8. How do viruses cause disease? _____

_____

_____

9. Circle the letter of the kind of pathogen that causes malaria.

a. bacteria   **b.** viruses   **c.** fungi   **d.** protists

▶ How Diseases Are Spread (pages 653–654)

10. List four sources of pathogens.

a. _____   **b.** _____

c. _____   **d.** _____

11. Circle each sentence that is true about how diseases are spread.

a. People cannot get pathogens by drinking water.

b. People can get pathogens by using a towel that was handled by an infected person.

c. Animals cannot spread pathogens to people.

d. Some pathogens live in soil or water.

SECTION 21-2 The Body's Defenses
(pages 655-661)

This section describes how the body protects itself from pathogens.

▶ Barriers That Keep Pathogens Out (page 656)

1. What is the body's first line of defense against pathogens? _____

_____

_____

_____

2. Complete the table to show the three different ways the body keeps out pathogens.

Barriers Against Pathogens	
Barrier	**How It Works**
Skin	
Breathing passages	
Mouth and stomach	

▶ General Defenses (pages 656–657)

3. The second line of defense in the body is the

_____, which occurs when body cells are damaged.

4. What happens in the inflammatory response? _____

_____

_____

CHAPTER 21, **Fighting Diseases** (continued)

5. The kinds of white blood cells that take part in the inflammatory

   response are called _____, which engulf pathogens and destroy them.

6. Why is the affected area red and swollen during the inflammatory

   response? _____

   _____

7. How does a fever help your body? _____

   _____

   _____

▶ **The Immune System** (pages 658–659)

8. The third line of defense against pathogens in the body is the

   _____.

9. List the two major kinds of lymphocytes.

   a. _____   b. _____

10. Complete the flowchart to show what occurs during the immune response.

   Immune Response

   ┌───┐
   │ _____ recognizes a pathogen.   │
   └───┘
                              ↓
   ┌───┐
   │ Some _____ attack and kill infected cells and the │
   │ pathogen. Others alert _____ to produce antibodies. │
   └───┘
                              ↓
   ┌───┐
   │ The pathogens are destroyed by _____ that bind to │
   │ the antigens on the pathogens.   │
   └───┘

11. What can lymphocytes do? _____

_____

_____

_____

12. What are antigens? _____

_____

_____

13. List three ways that antibodies help destroy pathogens.

a. _____

b. _____

c. _____

▶ AIDS, a Disease of the Immune System (pages 660–661)

14. What causes acquired immunodeficiency syndrome, or AIDS?

_____

_____

15. Once HIV enters the body, it enters _____ where it reproduces.

16. Is the following sentence true or false? Over time, HIV damages the immune system, and the body loses its ability to fight disease.

_____

17. Circle the letter of each sentence that is true about how HIV is spread.

a. HIV may spread from an infected woman to her baby through breast milk.

b. HIV is not spread by sexual contact.

c. HIV is spread by shaking hands.

d. HIV is not spread by using a toilet seat after it has been used by someone with HIV.

CHAPTER 21, Fighting Diseases *(continued)*

· ·

SECTION 21–3 **Preventing Infectious Disease** (pages 664–668)

This section describes two different kinds of immunity and some ways to stay healthy.

▶ **Introduction** (page 664)

1. The body's ability to destroy pathogens before they can cause disease is

   called _____.

2. What are the two types of immunity?

   a. _____   b. _____

▶ **Active Immunity** (pages 664–665)

3. When does active immunity occur? _____

   _____

   _____

4. Is the following sentence true or false? Activity immunity is produced by
   the cells of the immune system as part of the immune response.

   _____

5. How do memory cells keep a person from getting sick? _____

   _____

   _____

6. The process by which harmless antigens are introduced into a person's

   body to produce active immunity is called _____, or
   immunization.

7. What does a vaccine consist of? _____

   _____

   _____

▶ Passive Immunity (pages 666–667)

8. When antibodies are given to a person and are not made by the person's

   immune system, the person is protected by _____
   immunity.

9. Is the following sentence true or false? Passive immunity can last a

   lifetime. _____

10. How does a baby get passive immunity? _____

   _____

   _____

   _____

▶ Staying Healthy (page 668)

11. Circle the letter of each action that helps prevent infectious diseases.

    a. Share toothbrushes and silverware.

    b. Wash hands before eating and after using the bathroom.

    c. Cover your mouth when sneezing or coughing.

    d. Stay up late every night.

12. What three things can you do to help your body recover when you are
    sick?

    a. _____

    b. _____

    c. _____

13. A chemical that kills bacteria or slows their growth without harming

    body cells is a(n) _____.

14. Is the following sentence true or false? Some medicines don't kill
    pathogens, but help you to feel more comfortable while you get better.

    _____

CHAPTER 21, Fighting Diseases *(continued)*

Reading Skill Practice

Venn diagrams compare and contrast the features of two different things. Make a Venn diagram to show the similarities and differences between active immunity and passive immunity. For more information about Venn diagrams, see page 767 in the Skills Handbook of your textbook. Do your work on a separate sheet of paper.

· ·

SECTION 21-4 Noninfectious Disease
(pages 669-673)

This section describes three different diseases that are not spread from person to person.

▶ **Introduction** (page 669)

1. Diseases that are not spread from person to person are called

   _____ diseases.

2. Is the following sentence true or false? Over the years, infectious diseases

   have grown more prevalent. _____

▶ **Allergies** (pages 669–670)

3. What is an allergy? _____

   _____

4. Any substance that causes an allergy is a(n) _____.

5. Circle the letter of each item that people may be allergic to.

   a. pollen   **b.** some foods   **c.** some medicines   **d.** molds

6. Antibodies produced during the allergy response signal the body to

   release _____, a chemical that causes sneezing and watery

   eyes.

7. Is the following sentence true or false? If you have an allergy, the best thing to do is avoid the substance to which you are allergic.

_____

8. What is asthma? _____

_____

▶ Diabetes (page 671)

9. Circle the letter of the chemical that enables body cells to take in glucose from the blood and use it for energy.

  a. diabetes   **b.** allergen   **c.** insulin   **d.** histamine

10. The pancreas fails to produce enough insulin or the body cells aren't

using glucose properly in _____.

11. Is the following sentence true or false? A person with diabetes has low levels of glucose in the blood and more than enough glucose in the

body cells. _____

12. Circle the letter of each effect of diabetes.

  a. Never feel hungry   **b.** Lose weight

  c. Feel thirsty   **d.** Rarely urinate.

13. Complete the table to compare the two types of diabetes.

Forms of Diabetes		
Questions	**Type I**	**Type II**
When does it begin?		
What is wrong?		
How is it treated?		

CHAPTER 21, Fighting Diseases *(continued)*

▶ **Cancer** (pages 671–673)

14. What is cancer? _____

_____

_____

15. As cancerous cells divide over and over, they form abnormal tissue

masses called _____.

16. What are two causes of cancer?

a. _____

b. _____

17. Is the following sentence true or false? Surgery, drugs, and radiation are

all used to treat cancer. _____

18. Circle the letter of each sentence that is true about preventing cancer.

a. Avoid tobacco.

b. Expose your skin to sunlight frequently.

c. Eat plenty of fatty foods.

d. Visit the doctor regularly for medical checkups.

· ·

SECTION 21-5 **Cancer and the Environment**
(pages 676-678)

This section tells about different things in the environment that can cause cancer.

▶ **Chimney Sweeps and Skin Cancer** (pages 676–677)

1. What did Percivall Pott observe about chimney sweeps? _____

_____

2. Is the following sentence true or false? The environment has no effects

on people's health. _____

3. How can the risk of cancer caused by substances in the environment be

reduced? _____

_____

_____

4. What is the role of the Environmental Protection Agency, or EPA?

_____

_____

_____

▶ Environmental Carcinogens Today (page 678)

5. Complete the table to compare two kinds of carcinogens found in the
environment.

Environmental Carcinogens		
Questions	**Asbestos**	**Ultraviolet Light**
What is it?		
What kind of cancer does it cause?		
How does it cause cancer?		

Reading Skill Practice

A summary is a way to present information in a shortened, more concise form. Writing a
summary is a good way to review what you have just read. Write a summary for this section
about carcinogens in the environment. Remember to keep your summary short and include only
the important details. Do your work on a separate sheet of paper.

CHAPTER 21, Fighting Diseases *(continued)*

WordWise

Match each definition on the left with the correct term on the right. Then write the number of each term in the appropriate box below. When you have filled in all the boxes, add up the numbers in each column, row, and two diagonals. The sums should be the same. Some terms may not be used.

Clues

A. A chemical that kills bacteria or slows their growth without harming body cells

B. Consists of pathogens that have been weakened or killed but can trigger the immune system

C. The body's ability to destroy pathogens before they can cause disease

D. A chemical that destroys a pathogen by locking onto its antigen

E. A lymphocyte that identifies pathogens and activates B cells

F. A poison produced by bacteria that damages cells

G. An organism that causes disease

H. A white blood cell that engulfs pathogens in the inflammatory response

I. A disorder in which the immune system is overly sensitive to substances not normally found in the body

Key Terms

1. histamine
2. carcinogen
3. phagocyte
4. active immunity
5. antibiotic
6. immunity
7. toxin
8. T cell
9. antibody
10. pathogen
11. allergy
12. lymphocyte
13. vaccine

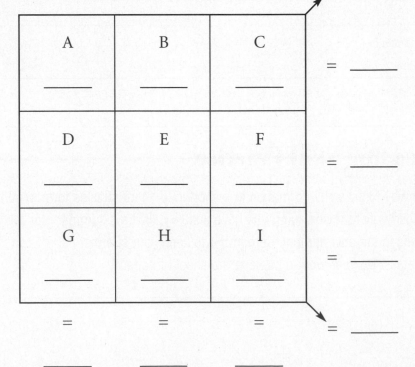

Science Explorer Focus on Life Science

CHAPTER 22
THE NERVOUS SYSTEM

SECTION 22-1 **How the Nervous System Works**
(pages 684-688)

This section describes what the nervous system does in the body. It also tells how nerve impulses travel.

▶ **Jobs of the Nervous System** (page 685)

1. List three jobs of the nervous system.

   a. _____

   b. _____

   c. _____

2. Is the following sentence true or false? You can move without your

   nervous system. _____

3. From what two places does the nervous system receive information?

   a. _____   b. _____

4. Circle the letter of a change in the environment that can make an
   organism react.

   a. response   **b.** stimulus   **c.** homeostasis   **d.** nerve impulse

5. Is the following true or false? All nervous system responses are voluntary,

   or under your control. _____

6. How does the nervous system help maintain homeostasis? _____

   _____

   _____

CHAPTER 22, The Nervous System *(continued)*

▶ The Neuron—A Message-Carrying Cell (pages 685–687)

Match each term with its definition.

Terms	Definitions
_____ 7. axon	**a.** The message that a nerve cell carries
_____ 8. dendrite	**b.** An extension from a nerve cell that carries impulses toward the nerve cell
_____ 9. neuron	**c.** An extension from a nerve cell that carries impulses away from the nerve cell
_____ 10. nerve impulse	**d.** A cell that carries information through the nervous system

11. Is the following sentence true or false? A neuron can have only one

axon. _____

12. A bundle of nerve fibers is called a(n) _____.

13. Complete the flowchart to show the path of a nerve impulse.

Path of a Nerve Impulse

The telephone rings. Nerve impulses begin when a(n) _____ in the ear picks up the stimulus of the telephone ringing.

↓

The nerve impulse moves to _____ in the brain. The _____ interprets the impulses and decides to answer the phone.

↓

Nerve impulses from the brain move to _____. The muscles contract in response, and you pick up the telephone.

▶ How a Nerve Impulse Travels (page 688)

14. The tiny space between each axon tip and the next dendrite or muscle

is called a(n) _____.

15. How does a nerve impulse cross the gap between the axon and the next

structure? _____

_____

· ·

SECTION 22-2 Divisions of the Nervous System
(pages 690-696)

This section explains the two major parts of the nervous system. It also describes what a reflex is.

▶ Introduction (page 690)

1. Complete the concept map to show the divisions of the nervous system.

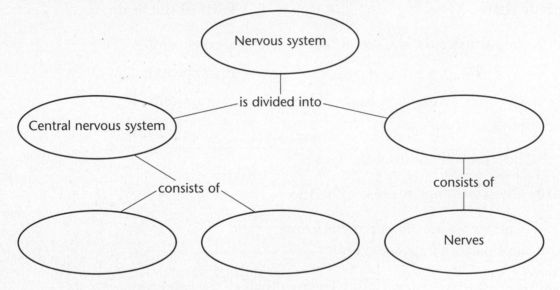

▶ The Central Nervous System (page 691)

2. Is the following sentence true or false? The central nervous system is

the control center of the body. _____

3. The part of the central nervous system that controls most functions in

the body is the _____.

4. The thick column of nerve tissue that links the brain to most of the

nerves is the _____.

CHAPTER 22, The Nervous System *(continued)*

▶ The Brain (pages 691–693)

5. Is the following sentence true or false? Neurons in the brain are only

interneurons. _____

6. What helps protect the brain from injury?

a. _____

b. _____

c. _____

Match the parts of the brain with their functions. Each part of the brain
may be used more than once.

Functions	Parts of the Brain
_____ **7.** Coordinates the actions of the muscles	**a.** cerebrum
_____ **8.** Controls involuntary body actions, such as breathing	**b.** cerebellum
_____ **9.** Interprets input from the senses	**c.** brainstem
_____ **10.** Gives the body its sense of balance	
_____ **11.** Carries out learning, remembering, and making judgements	

12. Is the following sentence true or false? The right half of the cerebrum

controls the right side of the body. _____

13. Creativity and artistic ability are usually associated with the

_____ side of the cerebrum.

▶ The Spinal Cord (page 693)

14. The spinal cord is the link between the _____ and the

_____.

15. What protects the spinal cord?

a. _____

b. _____

c. _____

▶ The Peripheral Nervous System (page 694)

16. What does the peripheral nervous system consist of? _____

_____

_____

_____

17. What is the function of the two groups of nerves making up the peripheral nervous system?

Somatic nervous system: _____

Autonomic nervous system: _____

▶ Reflexes (pages 695–696)

18. What is a reflex? _____

_____

_____

19. Circle the letter of each sentence that is true about reflexes.

a. In some reflex actions, the spinal cord, rather than the brain, directs the muscles to contract.

b. Reflexes protect you from getting hurt badly.

c. Nerve impulses move to the brain faster than they do to the spinal cord.

d. The reflex action takes longer than it does for you to feel pain.

▶ Safety and the Nervous System (page 696)

20. A bruiselike injury of the brain is called a(n) _____.

CHAPTER 22, The Nervous System *(continued)*

21. What can decrease your chances of getting a brain injury? _____

_____

_____

22. What happens when the spinal cord is cut or crushed? _____

_____

_____

_____

SECTION 22-3 **Light** (pages 698-701)

This section explains what the electromagnetic spectrum is and describes how light behaves.

▶ The Electromagnetic Spectrum (pages 698–699)

1. Sunlight travels to Earth in the form of _____,
a form of energy that can travel through space.

2. What is the electromagnetic spectrum made up of? _____

_____

_____

3. The part of the electromagnetic spectrum that you can see is called

_____.

4. Is the following sentence true or false? The longest wavelengths of

visible light are seen as red. _____

▶ The Behavior of Light (pages 699–700)

5. Is the following sentence true or false? Light usually travels in a straight

line unless it strikes an object. _____

6. Complete the concept map to show what happens to light when it strikes an object.

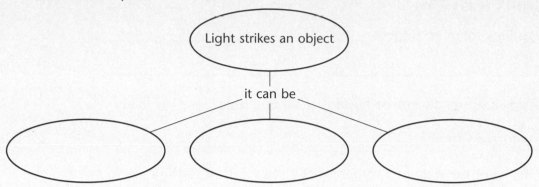

7. Is the following sentence true or false? Light-colored fabrics absorb

light. _____

8. What is reflection? _____

_____

_____

9. Circle the letter of each sentence that is true about reflected light.

a. The angle of incidence is the angle between the reflected wave and the imaginary line that is perpendicular to the surface.

b. The angle of reflection is always greater than the angle of incidence.

c. Regular reflection occurs when rays of light hit a smooth surface.

d. Diffuse reflection occurs when rays of light hit a bumpy surface and the waves are reflected at different angles.

10. Circle the letter of the material that allows light to pass through.

a. mirror **b.** dark fabric

c. glass **d.** pavement

11. Is the following sentence true or false? When light is transmitted from

one material to another, it stays at the same speed. _____

12. The bending of light due to a change in speed is called

_____.

CHAPTER 22, The Nervous System *(continued)*

▶ Using Light (page 701)

13. How does a lens form an image? _____

_____

14. Is the following sentence true or false? A telescope uses lenses to focus

light and record an image. _____

15. Circle the letter of the part of a camera that allows light into the camera.

   a. shutter   **b.** diaphragm   **c.** lens   **d.** film

· ·

SECTION 22-4   The Senses (pages 702-709)

This section describes the senses and how they work to tell you about your environment.

▶ Introduction (page 702)

1. What are the major senses? _____

_____

2. The sense organs change information about the environment into

_____ and send them to the brain.

▶ Vision (pages 703–704)

Match the parts of the eye with their function.

Parts	Functions
_____ **3.** iris	**a.** The layer of receptor cells that lines the back of the eye where nerve impulses begin
_____ **4.** lens	**b.** Regulates the amount of light entering the eye and gives the eye its color
_____ **5.** cornea	**c.** The opening through which light enters the eye
_____ **6.** pupil	**d.** The clear tissue that covers the front of the eye
_____ **7.** retina	**e.** Focuses light

8. Is the following sentence true or false? Cone cells work best in dim light and enable you to see black, white, and shades of gray.

_____

9. What two things happen to the image in the cerebrum?

a. _____

b. _____

▶ Correcting Vision Problems (pages 704–705)

10. Complete the table to show the two kinds of vision problems.

Vision Problems		
Questions	Nearsightedness	Farsightedness
What is wrong?		
What causes it?		
How is it corrected?		

▶ Hearing (pages 706–707)

11. Ears convert _____, a stimulus, to nerve impulses that your brain interprets.

12. How are sounds made? _____

_____

13. Is the following sentence true or false? Sound waves can travel only

through air. _____

14. The outer ear is shaped like a(n) _____ to gather sound waves.

15. Circle the letter of the membrane that vibrates when sound waves strike it.

   a. outer ear   b. hammer   c. anvil   d. eardrum

16. What is the cochlea? _____

_____

CHAPTER 22, The Nervous System *(continued)*

▶ **Your Sense of Balance** (pages 707–708)

17. The structures in the ear that control your sense of balance are the

_____.

18. Is the following sentence true or false? The cerebellum analyzes the

impulses to determine if you are losing your balance. _____

▶ **Smell and Taste** (pages 708–709)

19. Is the following sentence true or false? The flavor of food is determined

only by taste. _____

▶ **Touch** (page 709)

20. The largest sense organ is the _____.

21. Why is pain an important feeling? _____

_____

📖 **Reading Skill Practice**

Photographs and illustrations in textbooks can help you understand what you have read. Look carefully at Figure 19 on page 704. What idea does this photograph communicate? Do your work on a separate sheet of paper.

SECTION 22-5 **Alcohol and Other Drugs** (pages 710–718)

This section explains how drug abuse can affect the nervous system. It also describes how alcohol harms the body.

▶ **Introduction** (page 710)

1. Any chemical that causes changes in a person's body or behavior is a(n)

_____.

▶ Medicines (page 710)

2. What are medicines? _____

_____

_____

3. Is the following sentence true or false? It is not necessary to follow the

directions when taking medicines. _____

▶ Drug Abuse (pages 711–712)

4. The deliberate misuse of drugs for purposes other than medical ones is

called _____.

5. Circle the letter of each sentence that is true about drug abuse.

   a. Medicines can never be abused.

   b. Many abused drugs are illegal.

   c. The use of illegal drugs is not dangerous to the body.

   d. Abused drugs affect the body very shortly after they are taken.

6. The state in which a drug user needs larger and larger amounts of drugs

to produce the same effect on the body is called _____.

7. Circle the letter of the period of adjustment that occurs when a person
stops taking a drug.

   a. addiction   **b.** tolerance   **c.** withdrawal   **d.** depressant

8. Is the following sentence true or false? When a person is emotionally
dependent on a drug, the person is used to the feelings and moods

produced by the drug. _____

▶ Other Effects of Drug Abuse (page 712)

9. What legal and social effects do drug abuse have? _____

_____

_____

CHAPTER 22, The Nervous System *(continued)*

10. Is the following sentence true or false? If a person uses needles to inject a drug, that person has a chance of being infected with HIV.

_____

▶ Kinds of Drugs (pages 712–715)

Match the kind of drug with its characteristics.

Kinds of Drug	**Characteristics**
_____ **11.** depressant	**a.** Produces mood-altering effects when breathed in
_____ **12.** stimulant	**b.** Synthetic chemical similar to hormones used by athletes to improve performance
_____ **13.** inhalant	**c.** Slows down the activity of the central nervous system
_____ **14.** hallucinogen	**d.** Can make people see or hear things that do not exist
_____ **15.** anabolic steroid	**e.** Speeds up body processes

16. Look at Figure 27 on page 713. Which drugs do NOT cause emotional

dependence? _____

_____

▶ Alcohol (pages 715–718)

17. Circle the letter of the kind of drug that alcohol is.

    a. stimulant   **b.** depressant   **c.** anabolic steroid   **d.** inhalant

18. Is the following sentence true or false? Alcohol is the most commonly

abused drug in people aged 12 to 17. _____

19. Alcohol is quickly absorbed by the _____ system.

20. Is the following sentence true or false? If alcohol is drunk with a meal, it

takes longer for the alcohol to get into the blood. _____

21. Complete the table to show the effects of alcohol on the body.

The Effects of Alcohol	
Body System	**Effects**
Nervous System	
Cardiovascular System	
Excretory System	

22. How does the abuse of alcohol affect the body? _____

_____

_____

_____

23. A disease in which a person is both physically addicted to and

emotionally dependent on alcohol is called _____.

24. Is the following sentence true or false? Alcoholics must go through

withdrawal to give up alcohol. _____

▶ Avoiding Drugs and Alcohol (page 718)

25. What is the best way to avoid depending on drugs and alcohol?

_____

_____

26. Many teenagers begin using drugs and alcohol because of

_____ from people who are abusing drugs.

CHAPTER 22, The Nervous System *(continued)*

WordWise

Solve the clues by filling in the blanks with key terms from Chapter 22. Then write the numbered letters in the correct order to find the hidden question. Write the answer to the question.

Clues   **Key Terms**

A period of adjustment that occurs when a person stops taking a drug

— — — — — — — — — — —
1   2

Controls your body's actions that occur automatically

— — — — — — — — — —
    3

Carries impulses toward the cell body of a neuron

— — — — — — — —
        4

The layer of receptor cells that lines the back of the eye

— — — — — —
    5

Regulates the amount of light entering the eye

— — — —
   6

A drug that slows down the activity of the central nervous system

— — — — — — — — — —
        7

Another name for a nerve cell

— — — — — —
   8

The largest part of the brain

— — — — — — — —
9

The bending of light due to a change in speed

— — — — — — — — — —
  10

The opening through which light enters the eye

— — — — —
   11

The tiny space between each axon tip and the next structure

— — — — — — —
     12

Carries impulses away from the cell body of a neuron

— — — —
13

Hidden Question: _ _ _ _ _ _ _ _ _ _ _ _ _?
   1 2 3 4   5 6   7   8 9 10 11 12 13

Answer: _____

_____

CHAPTER 23

THE ENDOCRINE SYSTEM AND REPRODUCTION

The Endocrine System
(pages 724–728)

This section explains how the endocrine system works to control activities in the body.

▶ ## The Role of the Endocrine System (page 724)

1. What does the endocrine system control? _____

_____

_____

2. The endocrine system is made up of _____, organs that produce chemicals.

3. Is the following sentence true or false? Endocrine glands release their

chemical products through delivery tubes. _____

▶ ## Hormones (pages 725–726)

4. The chemical product of an endocrine gland is a(n) _____, or chemical messenger.

5. How do hormones affect the body? _____

_____

6. Circle the letter of each sentence that is true about hormones.

a. Hormones can regulate only the tissues and organs near the glands that produce them.

b. Nerve impulses from the brain can cause the release of hormones.

c. Hormones cause a slower, but longer-lasting response.

d. Any hormone can affect any organ in the body.

CHAPTER 23, The Endocrine System and Reproduction *(continued)*

7. A hormone interacts only with certain _____, cells that recognize the hormone's chemical structure.

Match the endocrine gland with the function of the hormone it produces. See *Exploring the Endocrine System* on pages 726–727.

Glands	Functions of the Hormones
_____ **8.** thyroid glands	**a.** Control the changes that take place in the body of a teenage boy
_____ **9.** adrenal glands	**b.** Trigger the body to respond to emergencies
_____ **10.** ovaries	**c.** Helps the immune system fight infection
_____ **11.** testes	**d.** Control the release of energy from food molecules during respiration
_____ **12.** thymus	**e.** Control the changes in a teenage girl's body

▶ The Hypothalamus (page 726)

13. Circle the letter of each sentence that is true about the hypothalamus.

    a. The hypothalamus links the nervous system and the excretory system.

    b. The hypothalamus is located on the kidneys.

    c. The hypothalamus sends nerve messages and produces hormones.

    d. The hypothalamus plays a major role in maintaining homeostasis.

▶ The Pituitary Gland (page 727)

14. What is the pituitary gland? _____

_____

_____

15. Is the following sentence true or false? The pituitary gland releases hormones in response to nerve impulses or hormone signals from the

hypothalamus. _____

Science Explorer *Focus on Life Science*

▶ Negative Feedback (page 728)

16. How does negative feedback work to control the amount of a hormone

in the blood? _____

_____

_____

_____

17. Complete the cycle diagram to show how thyroxine, a hormone
produced by the thyroid gland, is regulated by negative feedback.

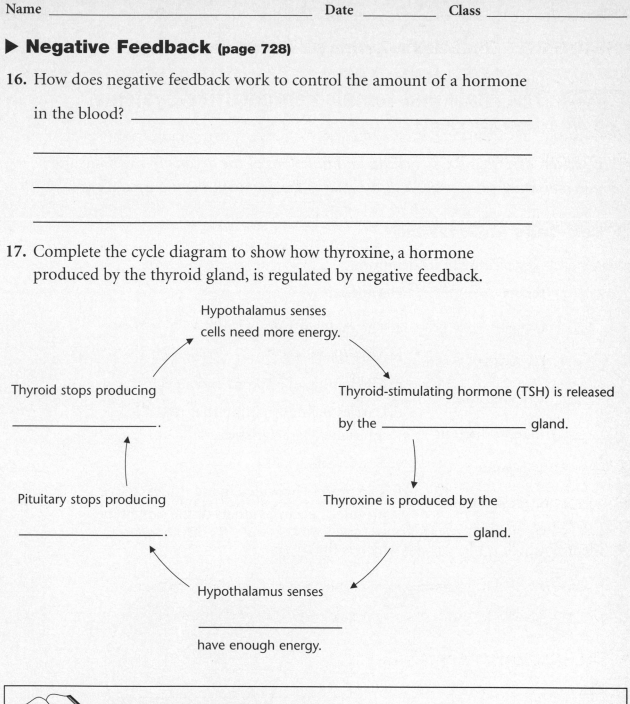

Hypothalamus senses
cells need more energy.

Thyroid stops producing
_____.

Thyroid-stimulating hormone (TSH) is released

by the _____ gland.

Pituitary stops producing
_____.

Thyroxine is produced by the

_____ gland.

Hypothalamus senses

_____

have enough energy.

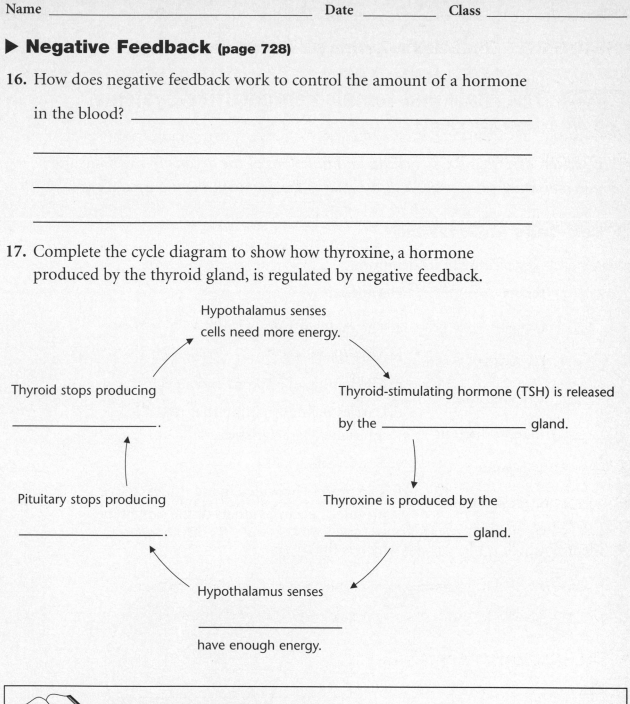

Reading Skill Practice

Knowing the meanings of the key terms in a section will help you to better understand what you
are reading. Make a list of key terms in this section. Write the meanings of these terms using
your own words. In this way, the key terms become a natural part of your vocabulary. Do your
work on a separate sheet of paper.

CHAPTER 23, The Endocrine System and Reproduction *(continued)*

The Male and Female Reproductive Systems
(pages 729-734)

This section describes the structures and functions of the organs in the male and female reproductive systems. It also explains the events in the menstrual cycle.

▶ **Sex Cells** (pages 729–730)

Match each key term with its definition.

Terms	Definitions
_____ 1. egg	**a.** The male sex cell
_____ 2. sperm	**b.** A fertilized egg
_____ 3. fertilization	**c.** The joining of a sperm and an egg
_____ 4. reproduction	**d.** Carries the information that controls inherited characteristics
_____ 5. zygote	**e.** The female sex cell
_____ 6. chromosome	**f.** The process by which living things produce new individuals of the same type

7. Identify which is the egg and which is the sperm.

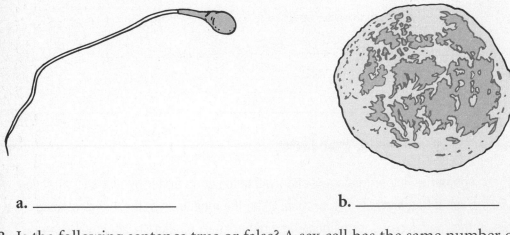

a. _____   b. _____

8. Is the following sentence true or false? A sex cell has the same number of

chromosomes as a body cell. _____

▶ The Male Reproductive System (pages 730–731)

9. What is the male reproductive system specialized to produce?

a. _____ b. _____

10. Circle the letter of the organs in the male where sperm are produced.

a. testosterone   **b.** testes   **c.** scrotum   **d.** penis

11. What does testosterone control? _____

_____

12. The testes are located in an external pouch of skin called the

_____.

13. Is the following sentence true or false? Sperm can develop normally only in slightly cooler temperatures than normal body temperature.

_____

14. What does semen provide to sperm?

a. _____

b. _____

15. Semen leaves the body through an organ called the _____.

▶ The Female Reproductive System (pages 732–733)

16. What is the role of the female reproductive system? _____

_____

_____

17. What do ovaries produce?

a. _____

b. _____

18. What does estrogen control? _____

_____

_____

CHAPTER 23, The Endocrine System and Reproduction *(continued)*

19. Complete the flowchart to show the path of an egg cell.

Path of an Egg

_____ produces an egg cell.

⬇

The egg cell moves through the _____ where it can be fertilized.

⬇

The egg enters the _____ where it stays to develop if it's fertilized.

⬇

An unfertilized egg begins to break down and enters the muscular passageway

leading to the outside of the body called the _____, or birth canal.

▶ **The Menstrual Cycle** (pages 733–734)

20. Circle the letter of how often an egg is released from the ovaries.

    a. daily   **b.** weekly   **c.** monthly   **d.** yearly

21. The monthly cycle of changes that occurs in the female reproductive

    system is called the _____.

22. What occurs during the menstrual cycle? _____

_____

_____

23. The menstrual cycle prepares the body for _____, the
condition that begins after fertilization has taken place.

24. Circle the letter of each sentence that is true about menstruation.

    a. Menstruation lasts about 28 days.

    b. Hormones of the endocrine system control the menstrual cycle.

    c. All girls begin menstruation at the same age.

    d. Women stop releasing eggs from their ovaries at about the age of 50.

● ●

SECTION 23-3 **Pregnancy, Birth, and Childhood**
(pages 735-741)

This section explains how babies develop before birth, what happens during birth, and what happens as babies develop into children.

▶ Introduction (page 735)

1. After fertilization, the zygote develops first into an embryo and then

   into a(n) _____.

▶ The Zygote (page 735)

2. Is the following sentence true or false? The zygote begins to divide to make two, and then four cells before it enters the uterus.

   _____

3. The growing mass of cells forms a hollow ball and attaches to the lining of the uterus, at which time the developing human is called a(n)

   _____.

▶ The Development of the Embryo (pages 736–737)

4. The membrane that surrounds the embryo and develops into a fluid-

   filled sac is called the _____.

5. What is the placenta? _____

   _____

   _____

6. What is the function of the umbilical cord? _____

   _____

   _____

   _____

CHAPTER 23, The Endocrine System and Reproduction (continued)

7. Is the following sentence true or false? Substances, such as chemicals from tobacco smoke and alcohol, can pass from the mother to the

embryo. _____

▶ The Development of the Fetus (page 737)

8. Complete the table to show the development of the fetus.

The Development of the Fetus	
Time in Development	**What Is Happening**
Nine weeks	
From fourth to sixth month	
Final three months	

▶ Birth (pages 738–739)

9. List the three stages of the birth of a baby.

a. _____ b. _____ c. _____

10. Circle the letter of each sentence that is true about birth.

a. Strong muscular contractions, called labor, enlarge the cervix so that the baby fits through it.

b. During delivery, the baby is pushed feet first out of the uterus, through the vagina, and out of the mother's body.

c. After delivery, the umbilical cord is clamped and cut.

d. After labor, contractions push out the placenta and other membranes into the vagina.

11. How does the baby's body adjust to the stress of the birth process?

_____

_____

_____

▶ Multiple Births (page 739)

Match the type of twins with its characteristics. Each type of twins may be used more than once.

Characteristics	Types of Twins
_____ **12.** Develop from a single fertilized egg	**a.** identical twins
_____ **13.** Develop when two eggs are released from the ovary and fertilized by two different sperm	**b.** fraternal twins
_____ **14.** Are no more alike than any brothers or sisters	
_____ **15.** Have identical inherited traits and are the same sex	

16. Is the following sentence true or false? Triplets and other multiple births can occur only when three or more eggs are produced and

fertilized by different sperm. _____

▶ Infancy (page 740)

17. Is the following sentence true or false? As a baby grows, its head grows more slowly, and its body, legs, and arms grow quickly to catch up.

_____

18. Circle the letter of the physical skill that babies develop first.

    a. crawl   **b.** grasp objects   **c.** walk   **d.** hold up their heads

19. Is the following sentence true or false? Babies can communicate only by

crying. _____

CHAPTER 23, The Endocrine System and Reproduction *(continued)*

▶ **Childhood** (page 741)

20. Circle the letter of each sentence that is true about childhood.

   a. Childhood begins at about the age of 13 years.

   b. Children become taller and heavier and become more coordinated.

   c. As they develop, children become less curious.

   d. Children learn to think about and care for others as they grow.

....

| SECTION 23-4 | **Adolescence-A Time of Change** (pages 742-747) |

This section describes what adolescence and puberty are. It also explains what changes occur during adolescence.

▶ **Introduction** (pages 742–743)

1. What is adolescence? _____

_____

▶ **Physical Changes** (pages 743–744)

2. The physical changes that occur during adolescence are controlled by

   _____ produced by the endocrine system.

3. What is puberty? _____

_____

4. Circle the letter of each physical change of puberty that occurs in girls.

   a. voice deepens   b. ovulation starts

   c. body odor increases   d. hips widen

5. Circle the letter of each physical change of puberty that occurs in boys.

   a. hips widen   b. sperm are produced

   c. hair grows on face   d. body odor increases

6. Is the following sentence true or false? All adolescents grow and develop at the same rate. _____

▶ Mental and Social Changes (pages 745–746)

7. Circle the letter of each sentence that is true about changes in the way teenagers feel.

    a. Teenagers cannot think beyond what's happening at the moment.

    b. Teenagers can think about the consequences of their actions.

    c. During adolescence, individuals begin to question things they once accepted as children.

    d. Teens usually don't wonder what they will do with their lives.

8. How do adolescents change socially? _____

_____

_____

_____

▶ Life as an Adult (pages 746–747)

9. Is the following sentence true or false? Adulthood definitely begins at the age of 18 years. _____

10. Circle the letter of the age when the process of aging begins.

    a. 20 years   **b.** 30 years   **c.** 40 years   **d.** 50 years

11. What changes occur to the body during aging? _____

_____

_____

_____

12. Is the following sentence true or false? The effects of aging can be slowed if people follow sensible diets and exercise regularly.

_____

CHAPTER 23, The Endocrine System and Reproduction *(continued)*

WordWise

Use the clues to identify the words for the puzzle. Write the words on the lines. Then find the words hidden in the puzzle and circle them. Words are across or up-and-down.

Clues	Key Terms
The chemical product of an endocrine gland	_____
The stage of development in which the developing human attaches to the lining of the uterus	_____
The stage of development from the ninth week of development until birth	_____
The period of sexual development in which the body becomes able to reproduce	_____
A fertilized egg	_____
The mixture of sperm cells and fluids	_____
The female organ that produces egg cells and hormones like estrogen	_____
The hormone in females that triggers the development of some adult female characteristics	_____

```
p  g  e  s  t  r  o  g  e  n  m  z
u  o  t  s  e  m  e  n  p  j  l  y
b  v  h  d  e  u  a  i  s  z  y  g
e  a  f  e  t  u  s  p  h  u  d  o
r  r  i  o  e  m  b  r  y  o  l  t
t  y  n  b  r  e  h  d  k  o  p  e
y  c  p  h  o  r  m  o  n  e  w  t
```

Science Explorer *Focus on Life Science*